S0-AYW-774

101 favorite stories from the BIBLE

101 favorite stories from the BIBLE

**Stories by
Ura Miller**

**Illustrations by
Deborah Hoerner**

TGS International is a division of Christian Aid Ministries, Berlin Ohio.

The Bible version used in this publication is the KING JAMES VERSION.

To obtain information or a catalog of publications, please contact:
TGS International
P.O. Box 355, Berlin, Ohio 44610, USA
Phone (330) 893-2428
Fax (330) 893-2305

This title is also available in Romanian, Russian, Spanish, Creole and German.

Assistant Editor
Naomi Lapp
Editorial Committee
Ura Miller, David Stutzman, Paul Weaver, David Troyer
Proofreaders
Wilma Dueck, Margaret Schlabach

Library of Congress Catalog Cardnumber
94-075773

ISBN 1-885270-00-3

Co-editions arranged by Angus Hudson Ltd.

Printed in Hong Kong

Table of Contents

OLD TESTAMENT

6

NEW TESTAMENT

The Old Testament

GOD'S WONDERFUL CREATION
In the Beginning

Themptholy Bible begins with God. He created the beautiful heavens above, and the earth below for us to live on.

There was a time when everything was dark, very dark. There were no living creatures to make a sound. No birds, animals, or laughter of little children were heard.

Then a voice spoke: "Let there be light" and there it was! God divided the light from darkness and named them day and night. This happened the very first day.

On the second day God started to prepare a beautiful world. He divided the water from the air. Then the blue sky appeared.

On the third day God made dry land by gathering the waters together. He covered the plains, hills, and mountains with grass, flowers, vines, and trees. Olives, apples, cherries, peaches, and berries grew on trees and bushes.

On the fourth day God put something red- orange and round in the sky. It was the sun. In the evening a glowing moon appeared and many stars dotted the sky.

On the fifth day there were sounds everywhere. What did God create this day? He made birds to fly in the air and fish to swim in the water. They were all kinds of sizes, shapes, and colors. Whales, gold fish, bluebirds, geese, and ostriches were only a few of the many creatures He created.

On the sixth day cattle, creeping things, and animals were seen. God made cows, horses, sheep, dogs, and cats, along with lions, tigers, bears, and rabbits. It was a wonderful birthday present for the very first man.

Do you already know the name of the first man? In the next story you will read about him.

On the seventh day God rested. He called it a Holy Day, having finished all His good work.

Genesis 1

A wonderful world created by God.

Parents: *Through faith we understand that the worlds were framed by the word of God.* (Hebrews 11:3)

Children: 1. Where does God live?
2. Who made all things that live?
3. Can you name some nice things that God made?

ADAM AND EVE
The First Man and the Mother of All Living

On the sixth day of creation, God's world was beautiful indeed. The fields were green, the flowers bloomed, and the birds and animals roamed the forests.

But there were no people, houses, farms, or cities on the earth. No children played under the trees. The world was ready for men and women to enjoy it.

Then God took of the dust of the earth and formed a man. He breathed into him the breath of life and the man became a living soul. God named this very first man Adam.

God had said, "Let us make man different from all the animals. He shall stand up, have a soul, and be like God. He shall be the master of all that is upon the earth."

In order to give man a home, God planted a beautiful garden in Eden, with a clear river flowing through it. Adam was to care for this garden. Then God brought to Adam the animals that He had made. He let Adam name each one.

But Adam was all alone in this perfect garden. God said, "It is not good for the man to be alone. I will make someone to be with Adam and to help him." So God caused Adam to fall into a deep sleep and took a rib from his side. From the rib God made a woman. Adam called her name Eve. Adam and Eve loved each other. They were very happy in this beautiful garden which God had given them for a home.

Genesis 2

Adam and Eve in the beautiful Garden of Eden.

Parents: *I will praise thee; for I am fearfully and wonderfully made.* (Psalm 139:14)

Children: 1. Who made Adam and Eve?
2. Who named the animals that God made?
3. In what garden did Adam first live?

THE GARDEN OF EDEN
The First Sin

For a time - we do not know how long - Adam and Eve were at peace in their beautiful garden. They talked with God as a man would talk with his friend. They did whatever God told them to do, and did not know of anything evil or wicked.

Yet Adam and Eve needed to learn that they must always obey God's commands. God told Adam and Eve, "You may eat the fruit of all the trees in the garden except one. If you eat the fruit of that tree you shall die."

Now among the animals there was a serpent, or a snake. Satan, that evil spirit who tempts us to sin, went into the serpent to tempt the woman to sin.

The serpent said to Eve, "You will not surely die. God knows that if you eat of the fruit you will become very wise and know what is good and what is evil."

Eve listened to the serpent. She looked at the fruit, thought of how good it would taste, and wondered if it would really make one wise. Ignoring God's command she took the fruit and ate it. Then she gave some to Adam, and he also ate.

After they had eaten they heard a voice. Although they knew it was God's voice, they did not come to Him as before. Fearfully they tried to hide themselves.

Because of their disobedience, God said to Eve, "You will suffer pain and trouble and be subject to your husband." To Adam, God said, "Because you listened to your wife when she told you to do what was wrong, you too must suffer by toiling and sweating among thorns and thistles."

Adam and Eve could not stay in their perfect garden home any longer. God sent them out.

Genesis 3

Adam and Eve sent out of the garden because of disobedience.

Parents: *As by one man's disobedience many were made sinners, so by the obedience of one shall many be made righteous.* (Romans 5:19)

Children:
1. Why did Adam and Eve hide from God?
2. Who made Adam and Eve leave the garden?
3. Why couldn't they stay in the garden?

15

THE FIRST FAMILY
Adam and Eve, Cain, Abel, and Seth

W hen Adam and Eve left the garden of Eden, they went into the world to live and to work. After a while God gave them a little child of their own, the world's first baby. They named him Cain. Then another baby was born whom they named Abel.

Cain liked to work in the fields and raise grain and fruit. Abel became a shepherd who enjoyed tending sheep.

While Adam and Eve were living in the garden they could talk with God as we talk with a friend. But now that they were out in the world they could no longer talk with God as freely as before. So when they came to God they built an altar of stone and laid something upon it as a gift to God. They burned the gift to show that it did not belong to them anymore. Now it belonged to God whom they could not see. They also prayed before the altar.

One day Cain and Abel each offered a gift upon the altar. Cain brought fruit and grain and Abel brought a lamb from his flock. The lamb that Abel offered was like the Savior that God had promised: gentle, patient, and innocent. So God was pleased with the worship of Abel.

But God was not pleased with Cain's offering. Instead of being sorry for his sin, Cain became very angry. He did not ask God to forgive him.

One day when they were in the field together Cain rose up and killed Abel! So the first baby in the world grew up to be the first murderer. He killed his own brother.

Later another son was born to Adam and Eve whom they named Seth. And to Seth was born a son named Enos. Then public worship began, with people calling on the name of the Lord.

Genesis 4

Cain and Abel each offer a gift upon the altar.

Parents: *God said, "Be fruitful, and multiply, and replenish the earth."* (Genesis 1:28)

Children:
1. What kind of work did Cain like best?
2. What kind of animals did Abel like?
3. Who became very angry and killed his brother?

NOAH THE ARK BUILDER
History's First Boat Ride

After a long while there were many people on the earth. Sad to say, they became very wicked. As God looked down from heaven he saw one good man whose name was Noah. God loved Noah. Because Noah was God's friend, God told him of the flood that he was going to send on the earth. God commanded Noah to build a big ark. God gave him exact details of how it was to be built.

No doubt the wicked people laughed at Noah for building this great boat where there was no water. But Noah kept right on building as God had commanded. He believed God's Word. Noah was also a preacher who spoke to the people about God and the punishment that was coming.

More than one hundred years later the ark was finished. God told Noah to come into the ark with his family of eight people. God caused animals, birds, and creeping things to enter the ark so that some of every kind of animals could be kept alive on the earth. When they were all safe inside the ark, God shut the door.

After seven days it began to rain. It rained for forty days and forty nights without stopping. The rain fell as if it poured out of great windows in heaven. The waters flooded the whole earth until there was no dry ground or breath of life left on it.

After many days the earth became dry again. God called Noah and his family to come out of the ark. Noah was so thankful to God for saving their lives that he built an altar of worship. There God formed a beautiful rainbow. He told Noah that the rainbow was a sign of His promise never again to destroy the earth with a flood.

Genesis 6 - 9

Noah and his family thank God for saving their lives.

Parents: *Thou art not a God that hath pleasure in wickedness: neither shall evil dwell with thee.* (Psalm 5:4)

Children: 1. Who told Noah to build an ark?
2. What was in the ark besides Noah and his family?
3. Why did God place a rainbow in the sky?

THE TOWER OF BABEL
The Beginning of Different Languages

The great flood that God had sent soon became a dim memory in the minds of Noah's children. Their families continued to increase until there were many people in the world. But the thoughts of their hearts were again becoming evil.

What was God's plan for families who wished to serve Him and do right? He did not want them to live close by those who did not love Him, but to spread out over the earth. Then they would more likely raise their children the right way.

As people travelled from the east, they found some level land. They said to each other, "Let us make brick and burn them thoroughly. Then let us build a big city with a very high tower in it. We will make a name for ourselves so that we will never be scattered."

So they began to build the city and the tower. At that time all the people spoke the same language. But the Lord came down from heaven to see this thing and it displeased Him very much. It was not His will that they all live close together in one place.

Then God caused men to speak different languages which they had never spoken before. Ever since that day many languages are spoken on the earth. Romanians do not understand English or Spanish. Germans cannot talk to Russians or Haitians until they have learned their languages.

The builders could not finish their city and tower because they were not able to understand each other anymore. They stopped the work and began spreading apart. Many of them went into other lands and spoke a different language. The unfinished city was named Babel, a word meaning confusion.

Genesis 11

The city and tower of Babel being built.

Parents: *He hath showed strength with his arm; he hath scattered the proud in the imagination of their hearts.* (Luke 1:51)

Children: 1. What was the name of the tower the people built?
2. Was God pleased with the people?
3. What did God do to stop them from building?

FAITHFUL ABRAHAM
The Friend of God

As time went on more and more people prayed to images made of wood and stone, called idols. They thought these images were gods which could hear their prayers and help them. These people did not call on the true God, or know His will. They did many evil things.

But the Lord God saw a different kind of man in the city of Ur. This man, Abram, prayed to the Lord. He always tried to do His will even though wicked people were living all around him. So the Lord said to Abram, "Abram, go away from this place. Leave your father's house and go to a place that I will show you. I will bless you and make you a blessing to others." Abram obeyed God, even though he did not understand.

Abram took his family, his tents, his flock of sheep, and his herd of cattle and left Ur. They crossed rivers and climbed hills until at last they came into the land of Canaan. This was the land God had told Abram about. There they lived in tents out in the green fields. Then the Lord came to Abram and said, "I will give this land to your children, and to their children, and it will be their land forever."

Then Abram built an altar and made an offering to the Lord. He worshiped God because he loved Him, served Him, and believed His promises.

One night God told Abram, "Count the stars, if you can, for so shall your seed be." Abram believed that God would give him many descendants even though he had no children.

Later God changed Abram's name to Abraham. He promised to give Abraham and his wife Sarah a son, a people, and a land. Abraham promised to serve God faithfully.

Genesis 12 - 17

Faithful Abram takes his family to the land of Canaan.

Parents: *By faith Abraham, when he was called to go out into a place which he should after receive for an inheritance, obeyed; and he went out, not knowing whither he went.* (Hebrews 11:8)

Children: 1. Who told Abram to leave home and go some where else?
2. Did Abram love God?
3. What did God tell Abram to count one night?

ABRAHAM OFFERS ISAAC
A Great Test of Love

One day God spoke to Abraham again, and said, "Fear not, Abraham. I will protect you from all your enemies, and reward you greatly for serving me."

Then Abraham said, "O Lord God, what good can anything do to me since I have no child to give it to?" Although Abraham did not know how God could keep His promise to give him a son, he still believed God's Word.

Finally, when Abraham was one hundred years old and Sarah was ninety years old the promised child was born. They named him Isaac as the Lord had told them to. Abraham and Sarah were very happy to have a little boy.

One day God said to Abraham, "Take now your only son, whom you love, and go to a mountain which I will show you. Offer him there for a burnt offering."

Though the command filled Abraham's heart with pain, he began to obey at once. With two servants and a donkey, Abraham and Isaac started northward.

On the third day Abraham and young Isaac went up on the mountain by themselves. There Abraham built an altar. He placed the wood in order, tied Isaac, and laid him on it. At last he raised his knife to kill his son. Just then the angel of the Lord called, "Abraham, do not hurt your son Isaac. Now I know you love God more than your son." What a joy and relief those heavenly words were to Abraham!

Then Abraham turned and saw a ram caught by its horns in the bushes. How thankful Abraham was to offer the ram instead of his son.

Genesis 15:1 - 2; 21 - 22

Abraham prepares to sacrifice Isaac.

Parents: *He that loveth son or daughter more than me is not worthy of me.* (Matthew 10:37b)

Children:
1. How old was Abraham when Isaac was born?
2. Who did Abraham love the most, God or his son?
3. What animal was offered instead of Isaac?

25

A WIFE FOR ISAAC
God Answers Eliezer's Prayer

After the death of Sarah, Isaac was lonely. Abraham wanted a wife for him, but he did not want Isaac to marry a girl from the people around them. Such a woman would worship idols, and would not teach her children the way of the Lord.

So Abraham called his most trusted servant, Eliezer, who took care of his silver and gold, his flocks, and his herds. He sent Eliezer far away to Haran. He wanted him to find a wife for his son Isaac among the people who worshiped the true God.

With ten camels and many presents, Eliezer started the long journey. Eliezer traveled with confidence because his master, Abraham, had told him that God would send an angel before him.

At last Eliezer neared the city of Haran. That evening he stopped to pray at the well just outside the city. He knew the girls would soon come to draw water. But how was he to know which girl was the right one? He decided to ask one of them to give him some water out of her pitcher. If she would answer kindly and say, "Drink, and I will give water to your camels also," he would know that she was the one whom God had chosen.

While Eliezer was still praying, a beautiful young woman came to the well with a pitcher on her shoulder. He asked for water and she answered with the very words he had prayed to hear. After she had provided water for all, the young woman said, "My name is Rebekah. Come to our house. We have room for you and your camels." Then the servant bowed his head and thanked God for his faithfulness.

The next morning Rebekah agreed to go home with Eliezer to be Isaac's wife. When Isaac saw her, he loved her and she became his wife. They were faithful to each other as long as they both lived.

Genesis 24

Eliezer's prayer is answered when he meets Rebekah at the well.

Parents: *The Lord is nigh unto all them that call upon him, to all that call upon him in truth.* (Psalm 145:18)

Children: 1. Why did Abraham not want Isaac to take a wife from their land?
2. How did God answer Eliezer's prayer?
3. Was Rebekah willing to go with Eliezer?

27

JACOB AND ESAU
Special Twins Are Born

After Abraham died, God was very kind to Isaac and blessed him. However, Isaac's wife Rebekah had no children for nineteen years. Isaac prayed earnestly and God answered his prayer.

Twin boys, Esau and Jacob, were born to Isaac and Rebekah. Esau grew up to be a hunter. He was rough and covered with hair. Jacob was quiet and thoughtful, staying at home and taking care of his father's flocks. Isaac loved Esau more than Jacob because Esau brought his father his favorite deer meat. Rebekah loved Jacob because she saw that he was wise and careful in his work.

In those days the oldest son in every family had what was called the birthright. This made him the chief among all the children. So Esau, as the older, had a "birthright" to more of Isaac's possessions than Jacob had.

Once when Esau came home hungry and tired from hunting, he asked Jacob for his soup. Jacob answered, "I will give it to you if you first sell me your birthright." Esau answered, "What is the use of the birthright? I'm almost starving." So he sold it to Jacob for a bowl of soup.

Isaac was now becoming feeble and almost blind. One day he said to Esau, "Go out into the field and hunt for a deer. Make me the dish of meat which I like best and bring it to me. Then I will give you the blessing."

Now Rebekah was listening and she wanted Jacob to have the blessing! She dressed Jacob in Esau's clothes, and put goat skin on his arms and neck, so that Isaac would think it was Esau. Then she sent Jacob into Isaac's tent with the meat that she had prepared. Isaac ate it and blessed Jacob instead of Esau.

Rebekah's plot had worked.

Genesis 25 - 28:9

Isaac is deceived by Rebekah and Jacob.

Parents: *By faith Isaac blessed Jacob and Esau concerning things to come.* (Hebrew 11:20)

Children:
1. What did Esau like to do?
2. Which of the twins did Rebekah like the best?
3. What kind of meat did Isaac like so well?

JACOB FLEES FROM HOME
God Comforts Him in a Dream

After Esau discovered that he had lost his blessing, he was very angry. He said, "Soon my father will die and then I will kill Jacob."

When Rebekah heard this, she said to Jacob, "Leave home and get out of Esau's sight before it is too late. Perhaps when he no longer sees you he will forget his anger."

So Jacob left home, beginning his long journey alone to Haran. One evening at sunset, he stopped to rest for the night. He took some stones for a pillow, and lay down to sleep. That night he had a wonderful dream. He saw stairs leading up to heaven from the earth, and angels were coming down and going up on the stairs. At the top of the stairs, he saw the Lord God standing. The Lord said to Jacob, "The land where you are shall be yours and your children's after you. I will take good care of you, and will bring you back again to this land."

In the morning Jacob woke and said, "The Lord is in this place and I did not know it! I thought I was all alone. This place is the house of God; it is the gate of heaven." Jacob made a pillar with the stones he had used for his pillow. He poured oil on it for a thankoffering to God.

Then Jacob journeyed on until at last he came to a well near the city of Haran. While waiting at the well he met Rachel, his own cousin. He was so glad that he wept for joy.

At that moment Jacob began to love Rachel. He longed to have her for his wife.

Genesis 27:46 - 29:14

Jacob dreams of angels and the Lord God.

Parents: *The angel of the Lord encampeth round about them that fear him, and delivereth them.* (Psalm 34:7)

Children:
1. Why did Jacob leave home?
2. Who went up and down the stairs in Jacob's dream?
3. Who stood at the top of the stairs?
4. What did Jacob use for a pillow?

JACOB WRESTLES WITH AN ANGEL

A Long, Long Lesson

While Jacob stayed in Haran, he wanted Rachel, the daughter of Laban, for his wife. Jacob told Laban, "I will work for you seven years if you will give me Rachel." Laban agreed.

On the day of the wedding the bride was brought to Jacob. As was the custom in that land, she was covered with a thick veil so that her face could not be seen. They were married, but later when Jacob lifted the veil, he found that he had not married Rachel whom he loved. It was her older sister, Leah, whom he did not love at all!

Jacob was very upset that he had been deceived, though he himself had deceived his father in much the same way. But Laban said, "In our land we do not allow the younger to marry before the older. I will give Rachel to you also if you work for me another seven years." Jacob agreed to do this.

After serving his uncle Laban for twenty years, Jacob gathered together his family and possessions and left Haran. On the way back to Canaan, he heard news that filled him with fear. He heard that his brother, Esau, was coming with four hundred men. Jacob remembered what Esau had said before he left.

That night Jacob divided his group and sent his family across a brook, while he alone stayed behind to pray.

While Jacob was alone, he felt that a man had taken hold of him. Jacob wrestled with this strange man until morning. The man was an angel of God. He blessed Jacob and changed his name to Israel.

When Israel met Esau, his brother, they made peace with each other.

Genesis 29:15 - 33:16

Jacob wrestles with an angel and receives God's blessing.

Parents: *The eyes of the Lord are upon the righteous, and his ears are open unto their cry.* (Psalm 34:15)

Children:
1. What was the name of the girl that Jacob loved?
2. Whom did Jacob wrestle with?
3. Who came with four hundred men?

DREAMS WITH SPECIAL MESSAGES

Joseph is Sold

After Jacob came back to the land of Canaan, his youngest son Benjamin was born. Now Jacob had twelve sons.

Of all Jacob's children, Joseph was his favorite. He loved Joseph because he was Rachel's child, and because he was the son of his old age. Joseph was also a very good boy, faithful and thoughtful. So Jacob made Joseph a coat of many colors. This was a special mark of Jacob's favor to Joseph. It made his older brothers very jealous of him.

One day Joseph said, "Listen to this dream. I dreamed that we were out in the field binding sheaves, when suddenly my sheaf stood up, and all your sheaves bowed down to my sheaf." His brothers answered scornfully, "Do you think that you will rule over us and we will bow down to you?" Then a few days later Joseph said, "I have dreamed again. This time I saw the sun and the moon and eleven stars all come and bow down to me."

Now Joseph's brothers hated him more than ever. They would not speak kindly to him. But his father gave much thought to what Joseph had said.

One time Joseph's brothers were taking care of their flocks far away from home. Jacob asked Joseph to go see whether all was well with them.

When Joseph's brothers saw him coming, they said, "Look, here comes the dreamer. Let us kill him." But Reuben pitied Joseph, and persuaded the others to put him into a nearby pit instead. He planned to later return him to his father.

While they sat down to eat their dinner a group of Midianite merchants came down the road. The brothers decided to sell Joseph to the merchants. So they sold their own brother for twenty pieces of silver.

Joseph was taken to Egypt by the merchants. He was very sad. His father Jacob mourned for him at home, not knowing what had happened to Joseph.

Genesis 37

Joseph is sold for twenty pieces of silver.

Parents: *Where envying and strife is, there is confusion and every evil work.* (James 3:16)

Children:
1. Who had a coat of many colors?
2. Why did Joseph's brothers hate him?
3. For how many pieces of silver was Joseph sold?

JOSEPH INTERPRETS PHARAOH'S DREAM

From Prison to Palace

A fter many days Joseph arrived in Egypt. How strange it must have seemed for him to see the great Nile River and the cities full of people.

The merchants sold Joseph as a slave to a man named Potiphar, an officer in the army of Pharaoh, ruler of Egypt. Joseph was a handsome boy, with a pleasant and willing spirit. His master, Potiphar, soon placed Joseph in charge of all his house.

At first Potiphar's wife was very friendly to Joseph. But when Joseph would not do wrong to please her, she became his enemy. To Potiphar she falsely accused Joseph of doing a wicked deed. Potiphar believed her story and had Joseph cast into a dark prison.

Joseph had faith in God and in prison he was cheerful, kind, and helpful. Soon, because of his faithfulness and honesty, the keeper of the prison put Joseph in charge of all the prisoners.

When Joseph was thirty years old, Pharaoh had a dream which troubled him greatly. One of his servants told him about Joseph.

Immediately Pharaoh called for Joseph and said, "I understand that you can interpret dreams." Joseph answered, "Of myself I am not able to do it, but God will give Pharaoh a good answer."

Pharaoh said that in his dream seven nice fat cows came up out of a river. Then seven poor thin cows ate up the seven fat cows, but they still looked thin, poor, and miserable.

Then Joseph said to the king, "Your dream means that there will be seven very good years, followed by seven very poor years. The king should appoint someone to store much food in the seven good years."

Right away the king appointed Joseph, and made him the second most powerful ruler in Egypt. God had not forgotten his friend Joseph.

Genesis 39 - 41

Joseph brings glory to God by interpreting Pharaoh's dream.

Parents: *Blessed is everyone that feareth the Lord; that walketh in his ways.* (Psalm 128:1)

Children: 1. Why did the people like Joseph so well?
2. Was Joseph able to interpret Pharaoh's dream?
3. Who told Joseph what the dream meant?

JOSEPH'S BROTHERS COME TO EGYPT

His Dreams Come True

When Joseph was made ruler over the land of Egypt, he began to do his work faithfully and thoroughly.

The seven years of plenty soon slipped by, then began the years of famine. Even in the land of Canaan food was scarce. But Jacob heard that there was corn in Egypt.

Then Joseph's ten brothers went to Egypt, and came to Joseph but they didn't realize who he was. As they bowed with their faces to the ground, no doubt Joseph remembered his dreams. He decided to treat them harshly to see if they were still as selfish and cruel as they had been. So he talked sharply to them, as if he were a stranger. He put them all in prison for three days accusing them of being spies. After this he kept Simeon in prison while the others went home. Joseph told them not to come back unless Benjamin, their younger brother was with them.

Soon the corn was gone and the brothers had no choice but to go to Egypt again. Once more the ten brothers all bowed to Joseph.

A dinner was prepared for them, and Joseph arranged the seating for his brothers. He placed them all in order from the oldest to the youngest. The brothers marveled. How could this foreign ruler know the order of their ages?

By this time Joseph's heart was so full that he could not keep back his tears. He hurried to his own room to cry.

After testing his brothers' honesty one more time, Joseph knew that they were no longer cruel and selfish. He sent his servants out of the room. As he cried aloud, he said, "I am Joseph your brother, whom you sold into Egypt!" Joseph, with love and tears of joy kissed all his brothers.

Afterward Joseph sent wagons and much food home with his brothers. He told them to bring Jacob his father, and all his family to live in Egypt.

Genesis 42 - 46

Joseph reveals himself to his brothers.

Parents: *This is my commandment: That ye love one another, as I have loved you.* (John 15:12)

Children: 1. Did Joseph's dreams come true?
2. Why was Joseph so stern with his brothers?
3. Did Joseph still love his brothers, even if they mistreated him?

MOSES IN THE NILE RIVER
A Basket in the Bulrushes

During Joseph's lifetime, the Egyptians treated the people of Israel kindly. Sometime after Joseph died, a leader who cared nothing for Joseph or the Israelites began to rule Egypt.

The king said to his people, "Let us rule these Israelites more strictly and make them work hard for Egypt." He was afraid that the Israelites would become too numerous and powerful. He commanded that all the Israelite baby boys must be killed.

At this crucial time, a lovely little boy was born to an Israelite family. For a while his mother hid him, but soon she had to make other plans for her active, noisy baby. How could she save him from the Egyptians? Surely God would provide a way. So she made a little "ark", or basket, from tall weeds that grew by the river. She covered it with pitch to keep out the water. Then she put her baby into the basket and placed it among the bushes at the edge of the river. She also sent her twelve- year- old daughter, Miriam, to watch close by.

Soon Pharaoh's daughter and her maids came down to the river to bathe, and they spotted the basket. The princess sent her maid to get it. When they opened it, the little baby began to cry. "This is an Israelite baby," the princess exclaimed. She loved him at once.

Then Miriam, who had been watching, asked if she should get a Hebrew woman to nurse the baby. The princess agreed, and Miriam ran for her mother.

When her mother came, Pharaoh's daughter said, "Take this child and nurse him, and I will pay you for it." So the mother happily took her child home again. There she taught him all the ways of the Lord.

When the child was old enough to leave his mother, the princess took him into her own home in the palace. She named him Moses.

Exodus 1 - 2:10

Pharaoh's daughter discovers baby Moses in a basket.

Parents: *By faith Moses, when he was come to years, refused to be called the son of Pharaoh's daughter, choosing rather to suffer affliction with the people of God, than to enjoy the pleasures of sin for a season.* (Hebrews 11:24 - 25)

Children: 1. What was the name of the baby who was put in the basket?
2. Why did his mother put him there?
3. Who found the little baby?

THE BURNING BUSH

A Voice in the Desert

Moses grew up among the Egyptians and learned all their wisdom. But in his heart he still loved his own people. The Israelites were now poor and hated slaves. Yet they served the Lord God, while the Egyptians worshiped idols and animals.

Moses felt a call from God to help the Israelites. When Pharaoh, the ruler of Egypt, heard about his efforts to free them from slavery, he became angry. Moses fled to another country when Pharaoh tried to kill him. There he became a shepherd.

One day Moses saw a strange sight. A bush was burning on the mountainside. Though it kept on burning, it was not destroyed.

As Moses approached the bush, the angel of the Lord appeared in the flame. A voice called, "Moses, do not come near; take off your shoes, for you are standing on holy ground."

Then God told Moses, "Come now, and I will send you to Pharaoh, and you shall lead my people out of Egypt." Moses replied, "What if the people ask, 'Who is this God? What is His Name?'" God answered Moses, "Say to them, the I AM has sent me, the One who is always living." But Moses wanted to see a special sign, so God performed two miracles. First, He told Moses to throw his rod on the ground. When Moses obeyed, the rod became a serpent. Next, God allowed Moses' hand to become diseased with leprosy. Then the Lord turned the serpent back into a rod and healed the diseased hand.

Still Moses was unwilling to go, because he thought he could not speak well enough. God answered him, "Am not I the Lord, who made man's mouth?"

At last Moses yielded to God's call. He went toward Egypt. On his way he met his brother Aaron. The two brothers came to the elders of Israel in the land of Egypt.

Exodus 2:11 - 4

God speaks to Moses from a burning bush.

Parents: *Thou shalt go to all that I shall send thee, and whatsoever I command thee thou shalt speak. Be not afraid of their faces: for I am with thee to deliver thee, saith the Lord.* (Jeremiah 1:7 - 8)

Children:
1. What did God tell Moses to do when he came near the bush?
2. Why did God want Moses to go back to Egypt?
3. What miracle happened with Moses' rod?

43

MOSES AND AARON SPEAK TO PHARAOH

A Battle Between God and Man

After Moses and Aaron had spoken to the people of Israel, they went to meet Pharaoh, the king of Egypt. They said, "Our God, the Lord God of Israel is calling us to worship Him. To do this we and all our people must go on a journey of three days into the wilderness."

Pharaoh became very angry. He said, "Moses and Aaron, what are you doing to call your people away from their work! Go back to your jobs and leave your people alone. I know why the Israelites are talking about going into the wilderness. It is because they are running out of work, so I will give them more work."

At that time the Israelites had been putting up brick buildings for the Egyptian rulers. They had been making their own bricks from clay mixed with straw. Up until then the Egyptians had been providing the straw for making bricks. Now Pharaoh said, "Let them make just as many bricks as before, but give them no straw." Of course this made the Israelites' backbreaking work almost unbearable. How could they ever find and gather enough straw, and still make as many bricks each day as before?

The Israelites became angry with Moses and Aaron. "We thought you would set us free, but now our suffering is greater!" they said.

Moses called upon the Lord, and the Lord said, "Go and speak to Pharaoh again and show him the signs I gave you." Pharaoh scoffed, "Who is the Lord? Why should I obey His commands?"

Then Aaron threw down his rod and it turned into a serpent. Pharaoh called his magicians. They also turned their rods into serpents. The Lord let them do this, but He caused Aaron's rod, in the form of a serpent, to swallow up the others. Still Pharaoh would not let the children of Israel go.

Exodus 5 - 7:13

Aaron's rod turns into a serpent and swallows the other serpents.

Parents: *I know that the Lord will maintain the cause of the afflicted, and the right of the poor.* (Psalm 140:12)

Children:
1. What were the Israelites making with clay?
2. Why did their work become harder?
3. Who did Moses call upon for help?

THE PLAGUES
Ten Wonders in Egypt

The Lord told Moses, "Pharaoh has hardened his heart and he refuses to hear my voice. He will not let my people go. In the morning, go stand by the river. When Pharaoh comes, wave your rod over the waters of Egypt."

Moses and Aaron obeyed the Lord. When Aaron struck the water, it turned into blood. All the fish died and a terrible stench hung over the land.

After seven days the Lord took away the plague of blood, but Pharaoh refused to repent. Next came huge numbers of frogs that covered the land. They were jumping around in the houses and everywhere else. But Pharaoh's heart just became harder.

Then Aaron struck the dust on the ground and everywhere the dust became alive with lice. The lice crept on the people and the cattle.

Next God sent great swarms of flies all over the land, so that the houses were filled and the sky was covered. But where the Israelites lived there were no lice or flies.

Then came a terrible disease that struck all the animals in Egypt. The horses, camels, sheep, and oxen died by the thousands. But no plague came upon the flocks of the Israelites.

After this Moses and Aaron took ashes from the furnace and threw them up like a cloud into the air. Instantly boils began to break out on man and beast. This was followed by a great hail storm, such as had never happened before in Egypt. Moses and Aaron often pled with Pharaoh, but he would not let Israel go.

After the hail storm came a strong east wind bringing clouds of locusts. The locusts ate up every green thing the hail had spared. Finally a thick darkness came that stayed for three days. The Egyptians could not see the sun, moon, or stars.

Then Pharaoh shouted at Moses, "Get out of my sight, and let me never see your face again!" Moses replied, "It shall be as you say."

Exodus 7:14 - 10:28

Egypt is destroyed by the plagues.

Parents: *Because sentence against an evil work is not executed speedily, therefore the heart of the sons of men is fully set in them to do evil. (Ecclesiastes 8:11)*

Children: 1. What did the waters of Egypt turn into?
2. How many days was it dark?
3. What did Pharaoh finally tell Moses to do?

THE PASSOVER
Freedom at Last

The Israelites lived in safety under God's care, while the Egyptians suffered destruction from the plagues.

By now many of the Egyptians feared the God of the Israelites and Moses, His servant.

Moses said to the people, "God will bring one more plague upon the Egyptians, and then they will let you go. Gather yourselves together in order by your families, and be ready to march out of Egypt. At midnight the Lord's Angel will go through the land, and kill the oldest son in every house. But your family shall be safe if you do exactly as I command you."

Every family was told to kill a lamb. They were to sprinkle the lamb's blood at the entrance of the house, on the door frame overhead and on each side. No one was to go out of his house that night, for it was the Lord's passover.

That night a great cry went up over all the land of Egypt. In every house the oldest son had died. Pharaoh the king of Egypt saw his own son lie dead, and knew that it was the hand of God. All the people of Egypt were filled with terror as they saw their children dead in their houses.

The king now sent a messenger to Moses. He said, "Hurry and get out of the land. Take everything you have and leave nothing. Pray to your God to have mercy on us."

So, early in the morning, the Israelites left Egypt after living there four hundred years.

The Lord God went before the large group of people. During the day time He formed a great cloud, like a pillar in front of them. At night it became a pillar of fire. It was a guide by day and a guard by night.

Exodus 12 - 13

The blood of a lamb protects the obedient from death.

Parents: *Christ our passover is sacrificed for us.*
(1 Corinthians 5:7b)

Children: 1. What did the Israelites put on the door top and
sides?
2. Why did they do this?
3. Who was to pass through at midnight?

49

THE RED SEA IS DIVIDED
Led by Pillar of Cloud and Fire

The children of Israel traveled toward the Red Sea, led by the pillar of cloud and fire. In a few days they came to the sea shore, with the water before them and high mountains on each side.

Meanwhile the Egyptian army was following them. Indeed, King Pharaoh wanted them back as soon as they had gone. So he called out his army, his chariots, and his horsemen, and followed the Israelites. Very soon the army of Egypt was behind the Israelites, and the people shook with fear.

They cried to Moses, saying, "Why did you bring us out to this terrible place? It would be better to serve the Egyptians than to die here in the wilderness!"

"Do not be afraid," answered Moses. "Stand still, and see how God will save you. The Lord will fight for you, and you will never see the Egyptians again."

Then the pillar of cloud went behind them and stood between the Egyptians and the Israelites. To Israel it was bright with the glory of the Lord, but to the Egyptians it was dark and terrible. All that night a mighty east wind blew over the sea. By morning there was a path of dry land with walls of water on either side of it. Then the pillar of cloud went before them. All the Israelites walked safely through the sea and into the wilderness on the other side.

The Egyptians followed with their chariots and horses. But now the sand had become muddy so that the horses and chariots were stuck fast.

By this time all the Israelites had passed through. Then Moses lifted up his hand, and the walls of water rushed back together again. All the army of Pharaoh was drowned in the sea, before the eyes of the people of Israel.

Then Moses wrote a song of victory, and all the people sang it together.

Exodus 14 - 15

The Egyptian army is destroyed by God's wrath.

Parents: *By faith they passed through the Red Sea as by dry land: which the Egyptians assaying to do were drowned.* (Hebrews 11:29)

Children: 1. How did the people know where to go?
2. Who made the cloud move?
3. What happened to Pharaoh's army?

GOD PROVIDES FOOD IN THE DESERT
Manna and Quail

Three days after leaving Egypt, the children of Israel came to a spring of water. They were very thirsty, but the water was so bitter they couldn't drink it. The people started grumbling. Moses asked God for help and God showed him a tree. Moses threw the tree into the water and it became sweet. The Lord God was always ready to help His people if they asked Him.

Later they came to an oasis where there were seventy tall palm trees and plenty of water. They stayed there for many days; it was their first time of rest since leaving Egypt.

As the Israelites traveled on, they complained time and again. They even said to Moses, "In Egypt we had plenty to eat. Now you and Aaron have brought us out here in the wilderness to die." Of course the Lord heard their ungrateful murmuring. He told Moses to tell the people that He would provide meat and angels' food for them.

The Lord did just as he promised. In the evening great flocks of quail came flying into the camp. The people caught and ate them.

In the morning the people saw the ground covered with small, white, round things that looked like frost. They had never seen anything like it before. "What is it?" they asked each other.

Moses told them, "This is bread from heaven which the Lord has given you to eat. Gather only as much as you need for today, and God will give you more tomorrow." The Lord wanted them to trust Him each day for their daily bread which was called manna. Some people disobeyed and kept some manna for the next day. The leftover manna was spoiled and had worms in it. However, on the sixth day of the week they were told to gather twice as much, for the next day there would be none. This was, of course, the Sabbath day. It was a day to rest and to worship God.

For forty years God provided manna day after day for his people.

Exodus 15:22 - 16:35

The Israelites gather manna sent to them by God.

Parents: *Man did eat angels' food: he sent them meat to the full.* (Psalm 78:25)

Children:
1. Were the children of Israel always happy?
2. What did Moses throw into the water to make it sweet?
3. What did the people call the food from heaven?

53

THE TEN COMMANDMENTS
Golden Laws from God

The Israelites came to a great mountain called Sinai. And the Lord said to Moses, "Go tell the people to wash themselves and be ready, for I will come down on the mountain to speak to them." On the morning of the third day, thunder and lightning shook the mountain, and a thick cloud covered it.

The Lord descended on the mountain and spoke to all the people the words of the Ten Commandments:

I.   You shall have no other gods before me.
This means that we must love God more than anything else.

II.   You shall not make any graven image, or bow down to it, nor worship it.
Carved images made from gold, silver, wood, or stone cannot save anyone.

III.   You shall not take the name of the Lord your God in vain.
God's name is sacred, so use it reverently when talking with God or man.

IV.   Remember the Sabbath day to keep it holy.
Think of God, do good unto others, and rest from all unnecessary work.

V.   Honor your father and your mother.
Obey your parents out of a heart of love.

VI.   You shall not kill.
Do not destroy people, because men and women, and boys and girls are made in God's image.

VII.   You shall not commit adultery.
A man is not to leave his wife and live with another woman, neither is a woman to leave her husband and live with another man. Keep yourself pure.

VIII.   You shall not steal.
If you have stolen anything, give it back or pay for it.

IX.   You shall not bear false witness against your neighbor.
Never speak a lie, but speak only the truth.

X.   You shall not covet anything that is your neighbor's.
We are not to wish for or strongly desire that which belongs to another.

Exodus 19 - 20:17

God speaks to the Israelites through Moses.

Parents: *There is one lawgiver, who is able to save and to destroy.* (James 4:12)

Children:
1. Where was God when He spoke to the people?
2. What are the ten rules called?
3. Who are we to love the most?

THE GOLDEN CALF
Trouble in the Camp

The Lord called Moses to come up on Mount Sinai again. He gave Moses two tablets of stone, upon which He had written the Ten Commandments with his own finger.

The Lord also showed Moses the pattern for a tabernacle, or church. The children of Israel were to build this for a place of worship during their travels.

While Moses was on the mountain with God, the Israelites asked a very wicked request of Aaron. They said, "Come now, make us a god that we may worship. As for Moses, we do not know what has happened to him."

Aaron did not have the strong character that Moses did, so he said, "Take off the golden earrings that are in your ears and bring them to me." Aaron melted the gold rings, and shaped the gold into the form of a calf. He brought out the calf to the people. Then they cried out, "This is your god, O Israel, that brought you out of the land of Egypt." Then Aaron built an altar and said, "Tomorrow shall be a feast to the Lord!"

Early the next morning they rose up and offered burnt offerings to the calf. They feasted, drank, and danced before the idol.

The Lord told Moses to hurry down to the camp, because the people have behaved wickedly. Moses pled with the Lord that He would not destroy His people. So the Lord spared Israel and sent Moses down to them with the tablets of stone.

Moses was deeply grieved when he saw the people in their wickedness, surrounding the golden calf. He threw down the two tablets of stone, breaking them to pieces.

Moses tore down the golden calf, burned it, and ground it into powder. He threw the powder into the water. Then he made the people drink the bitter water filled with the golden dust.

Exodus 31:18- 32:35

Moses is grieved by the wickedness of the people.

Parents: *Neither be ye idolaters, as were some of them; as it is written, The people sat down to eat and drink and rose up to play.* (1 Corinthians 10:7)

Children: 1. Who wrote the Ten Commandments on stone?
2. What animal did the people pray to?
3. What did Moses put into the water that he made the people drink?

AARON AND MIRIAM'S REBELLION
Trouble in the Family

The Israelites stayed in their camp at Mount Sinai for almost a year. During this time they were building the tabernacle, or church, and learning God's laws given through Moses.

Moses was the leader among the children of Israel, because the Lord had chosen him. He was more meek and humble than any other man on earth.

One day Moses' sister Miriam and his brother Aaron began accusing Moses. They complained that he had married a woman who was not an Israelite. They claimed that God had not only spoken to Moses but to them as well. Why couldn't they also be rulers over the people?

Had not Miriam watched over Moses when he was a little baby among the reeds? Had not Aaron and Miriam heard the grumbling of the people? Had they not seen God's miracles? In this way they were acting like naughty children jealous of each other.

The Lord heard what Aaron and Miriam said. He came down in a cloud and spoke to them from the doorway of the tabernacle. The Lord said, "Moses is my servant who is obedient in doing my will. I will speak directly with him. Why are you not afraid to speak against Moses?" Then the pillar of cloud rose up from the tabernacle because the Lord was very displeased with them. After it was gone, Aaron saw Miriam had turned white as snow with a serious disease called leprosy. God had sent it upon her as a punishment for their wickedness.

Greatly distressed, Aaron said, "We have sinned." He begged Moses to forgive them and pleaded for Miriam to be healed. Then Moses prayed earnestly to the Lord for her, and the Lord heard his prayer. God healed Miriam of her leprosy while she was shut out of the camp for seven days.

Then the people journeyed on toward Canaan.

Numbers 12

Aaron and Miriam falsely accuse Moses.

Parents: *Behold, the eye of the Lord is upon them that fear him, upon them that hope in his mercy.*(Psalm 33:18)

Children: 1. Did God hear the complaining of Aaron and Miriam?
2. Does God still hear when people complain?
3. Where was God when He spoke to Aaron and Miriam?

AFRAID OF GIANTS
Murmuring at Kadesh - Barnea

The Israelites came near the land of Canaan to a place called Kadesh - Barnea. Soon they expected to march into the land which was to be their home. God told Moses to send ahead twelve spies, to check out the land. At one place they cut down a cluster of grapes. It was so large that two men had to carry it between themselves on a staff.

After forty days the spies came back to the camp. They said, "We found it to be a rich land with grass for our flocks and plenty of water. We saw fields to raise grain, and many fruit- bearing trees. But we found that the people are very strong. They have cities with huge walls. Some of the men are giants, so tall that we seemed like grasshoppers beside them."

One of the spies, named Caleb, said, "All that is true, yet we need not be afraid to go up and take the land. God is on our side and He will help us overcome these people."

But all the other spies except Joshua said, "No, there is no point in trying. We can never take those walled cities, or overcome those giants."

They had already forgotten God's marvelous deliverance from Egypt. They forgot that He had kept them from the dangers of the desert. He had given them water from the rock, bread from heaven, and His law from the mountain.

All that night the people did not sleep. They blamed Moses and Aaron for all their troubles saying, "We wish that God had let us die in Egypt." Then they said to each other, "Let us choose a captain and go back to Egypt!"

But the Lord said to Moses, "How long shall this people disobey me and despise me! Not one of them who has murmured shall enter the promised land. No one who is twenty years old or older will enter except Joshua and Caleb, for they have always been faithful to me."

Numbers 13 - 14

The spies describe what they saw in the land of Canaan.

Parents: *As for God, his way is perfect: the word of the Lord is tried: he is a buckler to all those that trust in him.* (Psalm 18:30)

Children:
1. What did the spies carry back from Canaan?
2. Why were the Israelites afraid to go into Canaan?
3. Who were the two faithful spies?

61

A BRAZEN SERPENT
The Look of Faith That Counts

After many years, the Israelites again tried to enter the land of Canaan and searched for a route through a country called Edom.

Moses sent messengers to the king of Edom. They said, "Please let us pass through your country. We will do no harm to your land or your people. We will walk on the road, not turning to the right or to the left. We will not drink of your wells unless we pay for the water we use." But the king of Edom refused. So, they had to go around Edom.

While on this long detour, the people again found fault with Moses. They said, "Why have you brought us here? There is no water and no bread except for this vile manna, that we are tired of! We wish that we were all back in Egypt!"

Then the Lord sent poisonous snakes among the people. These were called "fiery serpents," because of the hot, violent swelling, and the thirst caused by their bite. Many people died from these snake bites.

Now the people saw their wickedness in speaking against Moses, for in doing this, they were actually speaking against God. Again they confessed their sin and asked Moses to pray for them.

So Moses prayed for the people, as he had so many times before. God heard Moses' prayer, and said to him, "Make a serpent of brass like the fiery serpents. Then set it on a pole where the people can see it. Every one who is bitten may look at the serpent on the pole, and he shall live."

Moses did as God had commanded him. After that, whoever had been bitten by a snake looked up at the brazen serpent and was healed.

Numbers 20:14 - 21:9

People are healed of their snake bites by looking at the brass serpent.

Parents: *As Moses lifted up the serpent in the wilderness, even so must the Son of man be lifted up; that whosoever believeth in him should not perish, but have eternal life.* (John 3:14 - 15)

Children: 1. How did God punish the people for murmuring?
2. What did Moses put on a pole?
3. What were the people to do to be healed?

THE DONKEY THAT TALKED
Balaam Stopped by an Angel

The children of Israel traveled to a land called Moab. The Moabites and their king, named Balak, lived there. Balak was afraid of the Israelites, so he sent for a prophet named Balaam to curse them. He wanted Balaam to ask God to send some great evil upon the Israelites.

Then the Lord said to Balaam, "You shall not curse these people, for they are blessed." But Balaam loved riches and honor. He was tempted to curse Israel for the silver and gold which he would receive from the king. So he left early in the morning on his donkey.

God sent His angel to meet Balaam on the road. Balaam could not see the angel but the donkey was able to see him. The donkey stepped aside into a field and Balaam hit him with his staff.

Soon the angel reappeared at a place where the road was narrow with a stone wall on each side. Again the donkey saw the angel and swerved away, crushing Balaam's foot against the wall. Angrily Balaam struck the donkey again.

Once more the angel of the Lord appeared to the donkey. He blocked the way at a spot so narrow that the donkey could not turn aside. When the frightened donkey fell down, Balaam was furious and again struck the animal with his staff.

Then the Lord caused the donkey to speak, and she said, "What have I done that you have beaten me these three times?"

By this time Balaam was so enraged that he never thought how strange it was for an animal to speak. He retorted, "I struck you because you will not walk where you should. If I had a sword I would kill you!"

The donkey spoke again. "Have I ever disobeyed you before? Why do you treat me so cruelly?"

Then God opened Balaam's eyes and let him see the angel with a drawn sword. Balaam fell on his face and confessed his sin.

Numbers 22

The angel of the Lord confronts Balaam.

Parents: *Which have forsaken the right way and are gone astray, following the way of Balaam, who loved the wages of unrighteousness.* (2 Peter 2:15)

Children:
1. Who made the donkey to speak?
2. What did the donkey say?
3. Why did Balaam get angry?

RAHAB AND THE SPIES
The Scarlet Cord That Saved

After Moses finished his work, the Lord called him up to Mount Nebo to show him the promised land. There Moses died and God buried him. No one has ever found his grave.

God called Joshua to be the leader instead of Moses. He ordered his officers, "Go tell the people to prepare food, for in three days we will cross this river Jordan."

On the other side of the river was the city of Jericho with very high walls around it. This city had to be won before the rest of the land could be taken.

Joshua sent two spies to check out Jericho. They came to the house of a woman named Rahab. She hid the spies so that no one would try to hurt them.

The king of Jericho found out that these strange men had gone into Rahab's house. So he sent officers to take them. But they could not find the Israelite men because Rahab had hid them under some stalks of flax on her roof.

After the officers had left, Rahab came to the two spies and said, "All of us in this country know that your God is mighty and terrible, and that He has given you this land. We heard how He dried up the Red Sea, and led you through the desert, giving you victory over your enemies. Because of this, our people greatly fear you."

"Now," said Rahab, "promise me in the name of the Lord that you will spare my life and the lives of all my family when you take this city."

The spies answered, "We will pledge our lives for yours. No harm will come to you, because you have saved our lives."

Rahab's house was built on a wall of the city. She let down a scarlet colored rope from a window. The spies said to Rahab, "When our men come, you must have this scarlet rope hanging out of the window. Then they will do you no harm."

That night the two spies slid down the rope. They found their way back to Joshua, telling him all that they had found.

Deuteronomy 34; Joshua 1 - 2

Rahab helps the two spies escape from Jericho.

Parents: *Let us hold fast the profession of our faith without wavering; (for he is faithful that promised).* (Hebrews 10:23)

Children:
1. Who buried Moses when he died?
2. Who was the Israelite leader now?
3. In what city did Rahab live?

JERICHO
City Captured Without a Battle

After the two spies had come back from Jericho to the camp of Israel, Joshua commanded the people to take down their tents and roll them up. He said, "Bring together your flocks and cattle, and be ready to march."

When Joshua gave the order, first the priests, then the rest of the people marched toward the river Jordan. The river was extra high and swift during this time of the year.

Joshua said to the priests, "Now step into the water." Then a wonderful thing happened. As soon as the feet of the priests touched the water, the river stopped flowing. Upstream the water piled up and downstream it flowed away, leaving a great dry place for the people to walk through.

At last the children of Israel were safe in the land that God had promised to them more than five hundred years before.

Then the Lord told Joshua how to take the city of Jericho. They could already see the thick, high walls around it. The Israelite army marched around the walls of Jericho once every day for six days.

On the seventh day, they got up very early in the morning. This day they kept on marching until they had walked around the city seven times. As they passed one window, they saw a scarlet rope. They knew this was the house of Rahab, who had saved the lives of the two spies.

When the seventh march ended, they all stood still. There was silence for a moment until the priests blew their trumpets. Joshua's voice rang out, "Shout, for the Lord has given you the city!"

When the Israelites gave a thunderous shout, they saw the walls trembling, crumbling, and falling!

In this way God gave them the city of Jericho. Rahab with her family was saved and blessed because she had faith in the God of Israel.

Joshua 3 - 6

The walls of Jericho crumble and fall.

Parents: *By faith the walls of Jericho fell down.*
(Hebrews 11:30)

Children:
1. How did the Israelites get across the river Jordan?
2. Who told Joshua what to do?
3. How did the Israelites know where Rahab lived?

69

GIDEON
Called to Deliver His Nation

After all that God had done for the Israelites and after Israel's promises to serve Him faithfully, surely they would never turn to idols, would they? Yet the people did forget their own God. They started worshiping the gods of Canaan which had not been able to save their own people.

Perhaps this idol worship was not so strange after all. As far as we know, the Israelites were the only people in the whole world at that time who did not worship images of wood and stone.

As the people began to neglect the Lord, and to worship idols, the Lord left them to suffer. He allowed the Midianites to rule harshly over them.

One day a man named Gideon was threshing wheat in a hidden place so the Midianites would not steal it. Suddenly he saw an angel under an oak tree. The angel said to him, "You are a brave man, Gideon, and the Lord is with you. Go out boldly and save your people from the power of the Midianites."

Gideon answered the angel, "Oh Lord, how can I save Israel? My family is poor and I am the least in my father's house."

Gideon thought that it must be the Lord in the form of an angel who was talking to him. So he brought an offering and laid it on a rock. The angel touched the offering with his staff. At once a fire leaped up and burned the offering. The angel vanished and Gideon felt afraid, but the Lord said to him, "Peace be unto you, Gideon. Do not be afraid, for I will be with you."

The Lord also told Gideon to set his people free from idol worship before he set them free from the Midianites.

On that night Gideon went out with ten men and destroyed the image of Baal. In place of it he built an altar to the God of Israel.

Judges 6:1 - 32

Gideon brings an offering to the angel of the Lord.

Parents: *And call upon me in the day of trouble; I will
deliver thee, and thou shalt glorify me.*
(Psalm 50:15)

Children: 1. What did the people use to make idols?
2. What did the angel do with Gideon's food?
3. Was Gideon a brave man?

AN ARMY FOR GIDEON
Three Hundred Chosen Conquerors

Gideon was a man of faith. He wanted to be sure that God was leading him so he prayed for God's special guidance to fight the Midianites.

The Lord said to Gideon, "Your army is too large. Send home all those who are fearful." When Gideon told the Israelites this, twenty- two thousand men went away, leaving only ten thousand.

But the Lord said to Gideon, "There are still too many people. Bring the soldiers down to the water where I will show you how to find the men whom you need."

When the men were beside the water, Gideon noticed how they drank. As they came to the water, most of the men knelt down to drink, laying aside their shield and spear. But a few men did not stop to take a long drink of water. Holding spear and shield in one hand, they caught up a handful of the water. Quickly they marched on, lapping up the water as they went.

God said to Gideon, "Set the men apart who lapped up the water. I have chosen these three hundred men to set Israel free. They are watchful men ready to meet the enemy."

Gideon saw the Midianites spread out through the valley like hordes of grasshoppers. He waited until it was night. Then he gave each man a trumpet and a pitcher with a lighted lamp inside.

Gideon told all the men to shout, "The sword of the Lord and of Gideon." They blew the trumpets and shouted and broke the pitchers in their hands.

The Midianites awoke to find lights all around them. In great terror they began to flee, running into each other in their panic.

So Gideon with his three hundred men gained a miraculous victory.

Judges 7

The Lord shows Gideon which men to choose for his army.

Parents: *It is better to trust in the Lord than to put confidence in man.* (Psalm 118:8)

Children:
1. Did Gideon need many or only a few men to gain the victory?
2. How did Gideon know which men to take?
3. Was Gideon a faithful man?

SAMSON
The Strongest Man Who Ever Lived

Many years after the time of Gideon, the people of Israel again began to worship idols. To correct them, God allowed their enemies, the Philistines to rule over them. But one Israelite man, Manoah, and his wife feared the Lord. At that time they had no children. But one day an angel came to the woman and said, "You shall have a son. When he grows up he will begin to save Israel from the Philistines."

The child was born, and was named Samson. He grew up to be the strongest man who ever lived. He remained strong as long as he obeyed God's commands to drink no wine and to cut none of his hair.

One day a young lion roared at him, but Samson was not afraid. He took hold of the lion and killed it with his bare hands.

Another time while Samson was in a Philistine city, they closed the great high city gate. They said, "Now we have caught him!" But that night he picked up the huge gate and carried it to the top of a hill.

After a while Samson loved a Philistine woman named Delilah. The Philistines offered her money if she would find out what made him so strong. For many days she begged him to tell his secret. Finally one day, Samson told this wicked woman everything: "If my hair were to be cut, God would take away my strength." While he slept the Philistines cut his hair, took him to prison, and poked out his eyes!

Sometime later many Philistines gathered in the temple of their god for a big feast. They brought Samson from prison to make fun of him. Samson put his arms around two strong pillars and prayed to the Lord for strength. Then he broke the pillars and the temple crashed to the ground. It killed more than three thousand men and women. Samson was also killed.

But Samson had done one last work for God. For twenty years he had subdued the enemy of God's people.

Judges 13- 16

Samson destroys the Philistine temple.

Parents: *Wisdom is better than strength.* (Ecclesiastes 9:16)

Children: 1. What was Samson not to drink?
2. What wild animal did Samson kill by hand?
3. What happened that Samson lost his strength?

RUTH
Your God Shall be my God

I n the stories we have seen the obedience of Joshua, the courage of Gideon, and the strength of Samson. But now during the time when the judges ruled Israel comes the sweetest story of all. This is the story of a girl named Ruth. Ruth lived in the country of Moab where the people worshiped idols.

Meanwhile in Bethlehem of Judah lived a man named Elimelech. His wife's name was Naomi, and their two sons were Mahlon and Chilion. For some years the crops were poor and food became scarce. So Elimelech took his family to Moab.

Elimelech had planned to return to Judah after awhile, but died while still in Moab. His two sons married women of Moab, one named Orpah and the other Ruth. The two young men also died, so Naomi and her two daughters- in- law were all left widows.

After ten years in Moab, Naomi heard that the Lord had again provided a good harvest in Israel. So she began getting ready to travel to Bethlehem. Her two daughters- in- law loved her and wanted to go with her.

Naomi said to them, "Go back to your own mothers' homes and may the Lord deal kindly with you." Then Naomi kissed them farewell and the three women all wept together. The two young widows said, "You have been a good mother to us; we will go with you and live among your people." "No, no," said Naomi, "You are young and I am old. Go back and be happy among your own people."

Then Orpah kissed Naomi and went back to her people. But Ruth would not leave her. She said, "Do not ask me to go, for I will never leave you. Where you go, I will go. Your people shall be my people, and your God shall be my God. Nothing but death itself shall part you and me." When Naomi saw that Ruth would not change her mind she stopped trying to persuade her. So the two went together toward Bethlehem.

Ruth 1:1 - 18

Orpah returns to her people but Ruth refuses to leave Naomi.

Parents: *But as for me and my house, we will serve the Lord.* (Joshua 24:15b)

Children:
1. Where did Orpah go after she kissed Naomi?
2. What did Ruth say to Naomi?
3. To what city did Naomi and Ruth go?

REWARDS FOR RUTH
The Great Grandmother of King David

When Naomi and Ruth arrived in Bethlehem, Naomi's former friends were very glad to see her again. It was just at the beginning of barley harvest. Ruth wanted to go out into the fields to gather grain which the reapers had left. This grain was to be food for herself and Naomi, for they were very poor. Soon Ruth came to the field of Boaz who was a relative of Naomi. He was a rich and well known man.

Boaz came out from the city to see his men reaping and said to them, "The Lord be with you." They answered him, "The Lord bless you." Boaz said to the master of his reapers, "Who is this young woman I see gleaning in the field?"

The man answered, "It is the young woman from Moab who came with Naomi. She asked to glean and has been here since yesterday."

Boaz said to Ruth, "Listen to me, my daughter. I have heard how true you have been to your mother- in- law Naomi. You left your own people who worship idols and came to Canaan to serve the Lord. Stay here with my young women and do not go to any other field. When you are thirsty, go and drink at our water pots."

Then Ruth bowed to Boaz and thanked him for his kindness.

At the end of barley harvest, Boaz held a feast on the threshing floor. In obedience to Naomi, Ruth went to him and said, "You are a near relative of my husband and his father, Elimelech. Will you not do good to us for his sake?"

When Boaz saw Ruth he loved her. Soon after this he married her. Boaz and Ruth had a son whom they named Obed.

Later Obed had a son Jesse. Jesse was the father of David the king.

So Ruth, the young woman of Moab who chose the people and the God of Israel, became the "Mother of Kings."

Ruth 1:19 - 4:22

Ruth gathers grain in the field of Boaz.

Parents: *Blessed is he that considereth the poor; the Lord will deliver him in time of trouble.* (Psalm 41:1)

Children:
1. What was the name of the rich man?
2. In whose field did Ruth glean?
3. What kind of grain were they harvesting?

SAMUEL

A Boy Lent to God

A new judge named Eli ruled Israel. He was also the priest or minister at the tabernacle (church), where the people came to worship.

About fifteen miles from the tabernacle lived a man named Elkanah. He had two wives, as many men did at that time. One of these wives had children, but the other wife, named Hannah, had no child.

Hannah poured out her heart to the Lord in prayer: "O Lord, if you will give me a son, he will belong to you as long as he lives."

The Lord heard Hannah's prayer and gave her a little boy. She called him Samuel, which means, "asked of God". While he was still a child she brought him to Eli the priest and said, "My lord, I am the woman who came here to pray. I asked God for this child. Let him stay here with you and grow up in God's house."

As Samuel grew he helped Eli more and more in the work of the Lord's house. He lit the lamps and opened the doors. He prepared the incense and waited on Eli, who was now growing old and was almost blind.

The children of Israel were longing for the time when God would again speak to His people. They remembered how He had spoken to Moses, Joshua, and Gideon.

When Samuel became a man, he began to travel among the Israelites. He gave God's Word to the people everywhere. His message was, "If you will come back to the Lord with all your heart, and put away the false gods, God will set you free from the Philistines."

The people obeyed Samuel and got rid of their images of Baal. The next time the Philistines threatened Israel, Samuel prayed. God answered his prayer and struck down the Philistines with a great storm of lightning and thunder.

Samuel lived to lead Israel for many years. The people trusted him, because he ruled wisely in righteousness.

1 Samuel 1 - 3; 7

Samuel is brought to Eli the priest at the temple.

Parents: *The Lord knoweth the way of the righteous; but the way of the ungodly shall perish.* (Psalm 1:6)

Children: 1. What was the priest's name?
2. What did Hannah pray for?
3. Did God answer her prayer?

ISRAEL DEMANDS A KING
God's Warning Unheeded

The wise prophet Samuel was now growing old. The elders of Israel came to his home and said, "You are old and your sons do not rule well. Choose a king for us like all the other countries have."

This request grieved Samuel because Israel already had a King, the Lord God. What more could they want. When Samuel prayed earnestly, the Lord answered, "Give the people their request. They have not rejected you, but they have rejected Me from ruling over them. But go and tell them of the hardship their king will bring them."

So Samuel told the men of Israel, "Your king will take your sons to be his soldiers and horsemen and to make weapons of war. He will take your daughters to be candy makers, cooks, and bakers in his palace. The best of your fields, vineyards, and olive yards will be given to his servants. He will take one- tenth of your sheep. Then you will cry because of the hardship that your king has brought upon you, but the Lord will not hear you."

Still the people said, "We will have a king so that we are like other nations." They wished to be a great people, to be strong in war, and to have riches and power. But God wanted Israel to be a quiet, peace loving people. He wanted them to live simply and to serve the Lord without trying to conquer other nations.

Then Samuel sent the people to their homes, promising to find a king for them. How would Samuel find a king? What kind of person would he look for? Who would help Samuel?

1 Samuel 8

The elders of Israel demand that Samuel give them a king.

Parents: *But ye have set at nought all my counsel, and would none of my reproof.* (Proverbs 1:25)

Children:
1. Was God pleased that the children of Israel wanted a king?
2. What did God say that a king would do to them?
3. Who promised to find a king for them?

SAUL ANOINTED BY SAMUEL
Israel's First King

T all, handsome Saul seemed to be a noble young man of the tribe of Benjamin. He lived during the time when the Israelites were demanding a king. His father Kish was rich and very powerful.

One day some of their donkeys strayed away so Kish sent Saul with a servant to find them. After they had traveled far and searched a long time, Saul was ready to give up. He said to the servant, "Let us go home or my father will worry about us."

Then the servant said, "In the next city lives a prophet named Samuel whose words always come true. Let us go to him and give him a present. Perhaps he can tell us where to find the donkeys."

While trudging up the hill toward the city, some young maidens told them that the prophet had arrived there that day. At the city gate they met Samuel, but they did not realize who it was. Saul asked, "Can you tell me where the prophet's house is?"

Samuel answered, "I am the prophet. Come with me because tonight we are having an offering and a feast as a sacrifice to the Lord. Do not worry about the lost donkeys, because they have been found." That night at the feast, Saul was honored as a special guest.

The next morning Samuel took a vial of oil and anointed Saul saying, "The Lord has anointed you to be king over Israel. Go now and do whatever God tells you to do."

As Saul turned to leave, God gave him a new heart. The Spirit of the Lord blessed Saul with a true desire to live unselfishly for others and to serve God faithfully.

Some time later Samuel called together all the people of Israel. It was a public meeting to crown Saul as Israel's first king.

In this way, God brought to pass His plan for Saul's life. It took him from searching for his father's lost donkeys to ruling Israel and being their king.

1 Samuel 9 - 10

Samuel anoints Saul to be king.

Parents: *I will go in the strength of the Lord God.*
(Psalm 71:16)

Children: 1. What animals were lost?
2. Who became the first king of Israel?
3. To whom did God give a new heart?

DAVID THE SHEPHERD BOY
God's Search for a King

King Saul obeyed God for some time, but then he rebelled against Him. God told Samuel the prophet, "I have rejected Saul from being king. I will replace him with someone who will obey my commandments."

This made Samuel very sad. He wept and mourned for Saul.

The Lord told Samuel, "Weep no more for Saul. Fill your horn with oil. Go to Bethlehem and find a man named Jesse. I have chosen one of his sons to be king."

So Samuel went to Bethlehem and prepared a sacrifice. He invited Jesse and his sons to the service. When they had come, Samuel looked closely at Jesse's sons one by one. The oldest, named Eliab, was so tall and noble looking that Samuel thought, "Surely this young man must be the one whom God has chosen."

But the Lord said to Samuel, "Do not consider his face, or his height, for I have not chosen him. Man judges by the outward looks but God sees the heart."

After seven of Jesse's sons had passed by, Samuel said, "The Lord has chosen none of these." Then he asked, "Are these all the sons you have?"

Jesse answered, "There is one more. He is out in the field caring for the sheep."

"Send for him," said Samuel, "for we will not sit down until he comes." So after awhile came the youngest son, perhaps only fifteen years old. His name was David which means, "beloved." With his sparkling eyes and shining face, David was handsome indeed. As soon as David had come, the Lord told Samuel, "Arise, and anoint him. He is the one I have chosen to be the king."

From that day forward the Holy Spirit was given to David to enable him to do the work he was called to do. The Holy Spirit helped him to be wise and faithful, a man after God's own heart.

Even as a youth, David was already a person of great courage. He killed a lion and a bear when they tried to seize a lamb from his flock.

1 Samuel 16

David watches over his flock.

Parents: *There is no power but of God, the powers that be are ordained of God.* (Romans 13:1)

Children:
1. What was the prophet's name?
2. Who was Jesse?
3. Who did God choose to be the next king?

DAVID AND GOLIATH
Victory Over the Giant

While Saul was still king of Israel, the Philistines gathered for war against the Israelites. Their armies camped on two hillsides across from each other. Every day a giant came out of the Philistine camp, daring an Israelite to come and fight with him. Goliath, as the giant was called, was over nine feet tall. He was covered with heavy armor and sharp glistening weapons.

Meanwhile, David's father sent him to the Israelite camp with food for his three brothers who were in the army. While he was talking with them, Goliath's taunts again rang across the little valley.

"I am a Philistine and you are servants of Saul. Choose one of your men and let him come out and fight with me. If I kill him, then we will rule over you. But if he kills me, then you will rule over us. Come now, send out your man!"

When David heard this he demanded, "Who is this man that dares to defy the armies of the living God? I will fight this enemy if no one else does."

When Saul heard of David's offer, he told him, "You cannot fight this giant. You are very young and this man has been a trained fighter ever since he was young."

But David insisted, "The same Lord who helped me kill a lion and a bear will give me victory over this giant."

Then Saul offered David his own armor, but it was too large and uncomfortable. Instead David chose five smooth stones from a brook and placed them into his shepherd's bag. With his shepherd's staff and his sling, he stepped forward to fight Goliath.

Goliath was insulted that such a young boy with hardly any weapons should dare to approach him. He said, "Am I a dog for you to come after me with a stick?" Yet before Goliath could strike a blow, David felled him with one well aimed shot from his sling. Then he drew Goliath's sword and beheaded him. With their champion slain, the Philistines fled.

I Samuel 17

David conquers the giant in the name of the Lord.

Parents: *The Lord taketh pleasure in them that fear Him, in those that hope in His mercy.* (Psalm 147:11)

Children: 1. What was the giant's name?
2. What did David pick up at the brook?
3. What was David's weapon called?

DAVID'S WISE BEHAVIOR
Saul's Jealousy

David's victory over Goliath was a great turning point in his life. After this, he never went back to herding his father's sheep. King Saul took him into his own house and made him an officer among his soldiers. David was as wise and as brave in the army as he had been when facing the giant. Very soon he was in charge of a thousand men. Everybody loved him, both in Saul's court and in his camp. David had a spirit that drew all hearts toward him.

When David was returning from a great battle with the Philistines, the women of Israel joyfully came out of the city to meet him. As they were dancing, singing, and playing music, they said, "Saul has slain his thousands, but David his ten thousands!"

This made Saul very jealous and angry. A black cloud of depression hung over him as he imagined how David could be taking over the kingdom. Before this, whenever Saul had felt troubled, David's singing and harp- playing would soon make him feel better. But this time, in his madness, he would not listen to David's voice. Twice he threw his spear at him. Each time David dodged aside, and the spear hit the wall.

Saul decided to send David out on dangerous missions of war, hoping that the Philistines would kill him. Once he said to David, "I will let you marry my oldest daughter Merab, if you will fight the Philistines for me." But this scheme fell flat because Saul did not keep his word and gave his daughter to another man.

Then Saul found out that another one of his daughters loved David. Saul promised that David could marry her if he killed one hundred Philistines. Again he hoped that they would kill him. But once more David came home victorious, all the more beloved by his people.

1 Samuel 18

Saul becomes very jealous of David and attempts to kill him.

Parents: *He will bless them that fear the Lord, both small and great.* (Psalm 115:13)

Children:
1. Why did the people love David so much?
2. What did the women sing that made Saul angry?
3. What did Saul throw at David?

JONATHAN AND DAVID
Two Inseparable Friends

Saul knew that David had won the hearts of the people. So Saul asked his servants and his son Jonathan to help him get rid of David. But Jonathan loved David dearly for he saw how brave and noble David was.

One day Jonathan and David went out to a field. Jonathan took off his own royal robe, sword, and bow, and lovingly gave them all to David. He felt deeply grieved because his father hated David.

However, Saul would still seem friendly to David at times. So Jonathan and David decided to test Saul. They knew that Saul expected David to be present soon at a feast. Jonathan said to David, "Stay away from the king's table for a few days, and I will find out how he feels toward you. After three days I will come back here with my bow and arrows. I will send out a little boy near your hiding place and will shoot three arrows. If I tell the boy, 'Run, find the arrows. They are on this side of you,' then you can come home safely. But if I say, 'The arrows are away beyond you,' that means your life is in danger. You must hide from the king." Then Jonathan and David promised each other that they, their children, and grandchildren, should be friends forever.

At the feast Saul asked Jonathan, "Why isn't David here?" When Jonathan made excuses for David, Saul became so furious that he tried to spear his own son.

The next day Jonathan shot his arrows as planned. He shouted to the boy, "The arrows are way beyond you. Run and find them." After the boy left, David came out of his hiding place and ran to Jonathan. They fell into each others arms, kissed each other, and wept together. Now David knew that he must leave his home, wife, family, and friends, to hide from the madness of king Saul.

Then Jonathan went back to his father's house, and David searched for a safe hiding place.

1 Samuel 19 - 20

Jonathan gives David a warning not to come home.

Parents: *The Lord preserveth all them that love him: but all the wicked will he destroy.* (Psalm 145:20)

Children:
1. Who was Jonathan's father?
2. What did Jonathan give to David?
3. How many arrows did Jonathan shoot?

93

KING SOLOMON
Solomon Chooses Wisdom

During King Saul's life he could never harm David, because God protected him. Then Saul died and David became king. He ruled Israel wisely for forty years. "David is a man after my own heart," God had said. David's life proved these words true, for he always loved the Lord. Of course God always loved David also.

David's young son Solomon was hardly more than twenty years old when he became king of Israel. Solomon feared God and carefully avoided evil. When he prayed for wisdom and knowledge to judge the people, God honored his request. Solomon's sincerity pleased God.

King Solomon was soon put to the test. Two women came before him with their babies. One baby was dead and the other was alive. Each woman claimed the living child as her own. One of them said, "This woman's baby died during the night because she lay on him. She placed her dead child beside me while I slept, then she took my child."

But the other woman said, "That is not true. The dead baby is hers and the living baby is mine."

The young king listened to both women. Then he commanded, "Bring me a sword." When the sword was brought King Solomon said, "Cut the living child in two and give half of it to each woman."

Then the first woman cried out, "Oh my Lord, give her the living child! Do not kill it!"

But the other woman said, "Neither of us should have him. Cut him in two!"

Then Solomon commanded, "Give the living child to the woman who had pity on him, for she is his mother."

When the Israelites heard this account they marveled at the insight of this young king. They saw that God had truly given King Solomon wisdom and understanding.

1 Kings 1 - 3

King Solomon uses the great wisdom God had given him.

Parents: *If any of you lack wisdom, let him ask of God...and it shall be given him.* (James 1:5)

Children:
1. Was Solomon young or old?
2. Who gives people wisdom?
3. Was King Solomon a wise man?

A NEW TEMPLE FOR GOD
Happy Days in Israel

The most important work during Solomon's reign was the building of the house of God, called the temple. The site chosen for this beautiful building was in Jerusalem on Mount Moriah. During King David's reign, he had stored up much beautiful cedar wood, special stones, and fine linen for the temple.

King Solomon drafted over one hundred eighty- three thousand men for all this work. This included the stone- cutters who labored in the mountain quarries. Ten thousand men were sent to Lebanon every month to be wood- choppers. Various tasks were assigned to the captive foreigners, the Amorites, Hittites, Perizzites, Hivites, Jebusites, and others living in Israel. Thirty- three hundred men were overseers in charge of the work. Before each building stone and board was brought to the temple site it was cut to the right size. Each piece fit so perfectly that no hammer, saw, or any other tool was needed at any time in the temple during its construction. The great building rose quietly and peacefully.

In the same way, God works in nature as He causes grass to grow, trees to bud, flowers to bloom, and fruit to mature. Jesus likewise builds His church here on earth in a reverent and peaceable manner. He has made provision for us to be His living temple, a dwelling place for the Holy Spirit.

After seven years the magnificent temple was finished. Would God accept it? Would He honor it with His presence?

On the day planned for the temple dedication, King Solomon stood on a platform before the people. The people watched as he knelt down, reached out his arms toward heaven and prayed earnestly for God's blessing.

As Solomon finished his prayer, fire fell from heaven and consumed the sacrifice they had offered. The glory of God filled the temple, showing clearly that God was pleased. The people bowed on the pavement, worshiping and praising the Lord, saying, "He is good; for His mercy endureth forever."

1 Kings 4 - 8; 2 Chronicles 3 - 8

King Solomon prays for God's blessing.

Parents: *I was glad when they said unto me, Let us go into the house of the Lord.* (Psalm 122:1)

Children:
1. What did they call this beautiful building that Solomon built?
2. How many years did it take to build the building?
3. What did Solomon and the people do when it was completed?

ELIJAH
God Provides for the Prophet

Not long after Solomon's death, the Israelites started to worship idols. Some said, "Baal is the best god!" Others said, "No, Ashtoreth is greater." Still others proclaimed that the temple of Molech was the place to worship.

God hated this idolatry. He called Elijah, a man from the land of Gilead, to be a prophet who would speak God's Word to Israel. Elijah worshiped and obeyed only the true God.

The Lord was displeased with Ahab, the wicked king of Israel. He said to Elijah, "Go tell Ahab that I will not send any more rain for several years." This made Ahab angry at Elijah. So God sent Elijah to hide in the wilderness near a brook called Cherith.

Each morning and evening, the Lord sent ravens to give Elijah bread and meat. At first Elijah had enough drinking water from the brook, but it soon dried up for lack of rain. All the land of Israel was stricken with famine.

Then the Lord sent Elijah north to the city of Zarephath. He said, "I have commanded a widow there to care for you." As Elijah arrived at the city gate, he saw a woman gathering sticks. First he asked for a drink of water, then for a piece of bread.

The woman answered, "As the Lord lives, I have no bread but only a handful of meal and a little oil. I am gathering two sticks to make a fire. I want to bake a cake for my son and me before we starve to death."

Elijah said, "Fear not; go and do as you have said. But first make me a little cake, and afterward make one for yourself and your son. The Lord has promised that you will not run out of meal or oil until He sends rain again."

The widow obeyed, believing Elijah's word. From that day on the widow and her son had as much food as they needed. The Lord and His angels must have had a wonderful time as they kept filling those containers of meal and oil.

1 Kings 17

The Lord sends ravens to bring food to Elijah.

Parents:

Behold, the eye of the Lord is upon them that fear Him, upon them that hope in His mercy; to deliver their soul from death, and to keep them alive in famine.
(Psalm 33:18 - 19)

Children:

1. Why did Elijah hide in the wilderness?
2. How did Elijah get food in the wilderness?
3. How much meal did the widow have?

THE LORD GOD OR BAAL
Fire Falls From Heaven

A fter three years of drought in Israel, God promised Elijah that He would again send rain. He sent Elijah to King Ahab. When Ahab saw Elijah he asked," Is that you, you troubler of Israel?"

Elijah replied, "You are the one who is troubling Israel by your wickedness. Now gather together all Israel to Mount Carmel with the 450 prophets of Baal. There the people may decide whom they will serve, Baal or God."

Ahab obeyed and called everyone together on Mount Carmel. Then Elijah said, "You pray to Baal, and I will pray to God. The god who sends down fire on the altar will be the true God." All the people agreed.

The prophets of Baal tried first. All forenoon they prayed to Baal. They leaped upon the altar, cried aloud, and cut themselves with knives until their blood flowed. At noon Elijah taunted them. "Shout louder to get your god's attention! Perhaps he is talking to someone or is away on a trip or is sleeping."

All afternoon they raved, but there was no reply or answer whatsoever.

Then Elijah said to the people, "Come near to me." He repaired the Lord's broken altar and dug a ditch around it. He placed wood and a slaughtered bull on the altar. Then he asked that four large pitchers of water be poured on the meat and wood. This was done three times so that everything was soaked and the ditch was full of water.

Elijah prayed a prayer of only 63 words. Then fire fell from heaven. It burned up the sacrifice and the wood, the stones and the dust, and even the water in the ditch. This was no ordinary fire, for it burned from the top down instead of up from the bottom.

When the people saw this great miracle, they fell on their faces upon the ground. They declared, "The Lord, He is God! The Lord, He is God!"

1 Kings 18

God answers Elijah's prayer by sending fire from heaven.

Parents: *Thou shalt worship the Lord thy God, and Him only shalt thou serve.* (Matthew 4:10)

Children: 1. Did the prophets of Baal get an answer from their god?
2. Did God hear Elijah's prayer?
3. Where did the fire come from?

101

ELIJAH GOES TO HEAVEN
A Chariot of Fire

Elijah's work on earth was almost done. This was the great day when the Lord would take him to heaven in a whirlwind, for the Lord had revealed this to him. Elijah also knew that this would not happen until he had passed Bethel and Jericho, and had crossed the Jordan River.

Elijah had allowed a new prophet named Elisha to walk along with him. At every city they visited, Elijah urged Elisha to stay because God had sent him further. But each time Elisha replied, "I will not leave you." He was determined to go on with Elijah until God took him to heaven.

After leaving Jericho the two men walked about five miles to the Jordan River. Fifty curious young prophets from Jericho followed them at a distance. When they came to the banks of the Jordan, Elijah folded his cloak and struck the water. It divided instantly and they walked across on dry ground. Then Elijah asked, "What shall I do for you before I'm taken away?"

"Let a double portion of your spirit be upon me," answered Elisha. Elijah said, "You have asked a hard thing. Yet if you see me when I am taken from you, you will receive what you desire. If not, then you will not receive it."

Suddenly, while they were talking, fiery horses and a chariot of fire drove right between Elijah and Elisha and separated them. A whirlwind picked up Elijah and carried him into heaven.

When Elisha saw what was happening, he cried out, "My father, my father, the chariot of Israel and its horsemen!" Elisha knew that when Elijah left the earth, the Israelites had lost a man of more value and power than many horses and chariots. Now he could no longer see Elijah.

Elisha picked up the cloak that had fallen from Elijah. He struck the water of the Jordan, and it immediately parted as before.

Then the fifty prophets who had been waiting for Elisha came and bowed before him. They said, "The spirit of Elijah now rests on Elisha."

2 Kings 2

Elisha watches Elijah being taken to heaven.

Parents: *I have fought a good fight, I have finished my course, I have kept the faith; henceforth there is laid up for me a crown of righteousness.* (2 Timothy 4:7 - 8a)

Children:
1. Where did Elijah go to?
2. How did he go?
3. What did Elisha use to part the water?

A FAITHFUL LITTLE SLAVE GIRL
Naaman is Healed

I n the country of Syria lived a little slave girl who had been taken from her family in Israel. Her master was a great general in the king's army, but he had a terrible disease called leprosy. This little girl told Naaman's wife that he could be healed if he would go to the prophet in Samaria.

Naaman was desperate for help. So he set off, taking gifts of gold, silver, suits of clothing, and a letter from the king of Syria. The letter was addressed to the king of Israel. It said, "The man bringing you this letter is my servant. I want you to heal him of his leprosy." In Israel Naaman presented the letter to the king.

The king of Israel was very upset because of the letter. He demanded, "Am I God, that can kill and make alive?"

The prophet Elisha heard of the king's distress and invited Naaman to his house. So Naaman with his horses and chariot, drove to Elisha's house. He waited at the door but the prophet did not invite him in or go out to meet him. Instead Elisha sent out his servant to tell Naaman, "Go dip yourself seven times in the Jordan River and you will be healed."

This made Naaman furious. He had thought that he was great enough that Elisha should feel honored to come out to him, lay hands on his body, and pray. He could easily give up great riches in order to be healed but it was much harder to give up his pride.

God had seen the pride in Naaman's heart. He wanted Naaman to learn to be humble and obedient to Him. God also wanted men of all ages to know that He does not honor human greatness.

Naaman very nearly returned home a proud and angry leper. But his servants pointed out, "If the prophet had told you to do some great thing you would have done it. So why not do this simple thing?"

Finally Naaman was persuaded. He dipped seven times in the Jordan River and his skin became as healthy as a little child's.

Humbly Naaman declared, "Now I know that there is no God except the God of Israel. I will worship only Him."

Naaman dips in the Jordan River seven times and is healed.

Parents: *And he put forth his hand, and touched him, saying, "I will. Be thou clean." And immediately the leprosy departed from him.* (Luke 5:13)

Children:
1. How did Naaman learn about the prophet in Israel?
2. How many times was Naaman to dip in the Jordan River?
3. Was Naaman glad that he obeyed?

FOUR LEPERS FROM SAMARIA
God Delivers Israel From Famine

T he king of Syria led his mighty army into the land of Israel to war against them. They surrounded the city of Samaria, trying to force the people to surrender.

Day after day the food in Samaria became more and more scarce. The people became desperate for food.

One day a mother appealed to the king to enforce an agreement with a friend about taking turns to eat their sons. The king was shocked and horrified to learn that the situation was that terrible. He blamed the trouble on Elisha, vowing to behead him.

Then Elisha prophesied, "Tomorrow at this hour the siege will be ended. Flour and barley will be sold cheaply at the gate."

That evening four outcast lepers decided to risk entering the Syrian camp to beg for food. They said, "In the city we will die anyway. Maybe we have a better chance with the Syrians."

Before the lepers arrived in the camp, the Lord had already performed a miracle to fulfill the prophecy of Elisha. He had simply caused the Syrians to hear the noise of chariots, horses and a great army. They thought the king of Israel had hired the Hittites and the Egyptians to attack them. Filled with terror they fled, leaving their tents, horses, donkeys and all their food.

The four lepers found only a deserted camp. They helped themselves to food, silver, gold, clothing, and other treasures. Joyfully they stashed the things in a hiding place and returned for more. Then they stopped. "We must tell the king about this," they said. "We should not be selfish."

Before dawn the king was awakened with the news. He said, "This is just a trick to get us out of the city." Therefore several brave men were sent to look around. They found the way toward Syria littered with clothes and other things. The men were soon convinced that the Syrians were truly gone.

Then the people poured out of the city to pounce on the spoils of the Syrian camp.

2 Kings 6 - 7

The four lepers find food and treasures in the deserted Syrian camp.

Parents: *The wicked flee when no man pursueth, but the righteous are bold as a lion.* (Proverbs 28:1)

Children:
1. How many lepers were there?
2. Why did the Syrians run away?
3. How did the Israelites know the Syrians had fled?

107

JEHOSHAPHAT'S SINGING ARMY
A Choir Wins a Battle

Jehoshaphat was a wise and strong king of Judah. He served the Lord with all his heart. He got rid of all the idols in the land and sent priests throughout the country to teach the people God's Law.

Then Jehoshaphat heard that the Moabites, Ammonites, and Edomites had banded together against him. They were encamped with a great army near the Dead Sea. Because of this, frightened families from all the cities of Judah came together to seek the Lord. In utter dependence upon the Lord, they fasted and prayed at the temple, seeking an answer from Him. Jehoshaphat stood among them and led his people in fervent prayer.

Then the Spirit of the Lord came upon Jahaziel, one of the Levites. He said, "Do not fear this great host, for the battle is not yours, but the Lord's. Be faithful, stand still, and see how the Lord will save you." This brought great comfort to everyone.

Early in the morning Jehoshaphat praised God for the battle to be won that day. He asked the people about sending the choir ahead of the army. Everyone agreed and singers were appointed for the choir.

Have you ever heard of an army led by singers marching toward the enemy? Can you imagine hearing all those voices echoing throughout the valley!

At the first sounds of singing and praising God, Jehoshaphat set ambushes to attack the Moabites, Ammonites, and Edomites. The Ammonites and Moabites became so confused that they destroyed the Edomites, then continued destroying each other.

By the time the singing army arrived they found only dead bodies. There was no need to fight, just as the Lord had said. For three days they gathered the riches, jewels, and other spoils. On the fourth day they blessed their God and returned to Judah and Jerusalem with great joy.

2 Chronicles 20

The Lord gives victory to Jehoshaphat's singing army.

Parents: *Oh, give thanks unto the Lord, for he is good, for his mercy endureth forever.* (Psalm 107:1)

Children:
1. Was Jehoshaphat a good king?
2. Did he serve the Lord?
3. Who marched in front of the army?

109

ESTHER THE JEWESS
The King's Choice of a Queen

Esther was a Jewish orphan who lived in the land of Persia. Her parents, along with many other Israelites, had been brought there years before as captives.

One day the Persian governors, aides, and army officers came to the palace at Shushan for a long holiday. King Ahasuerus wanted to dazzle them with all his splendor and wealth. The final week of merry-making was spent on feasting and drinking royal wine.

Meanwhile Queen Vashti also gave a party for the women of the palace. On the last day of the feast she received a royal summons. The king, giddy from all the wine, wanted to show off her beauty to the men with him. Queen Vashti did not want to disgrace herself in this way. She refused to come to the king.

This made the king furious. He asked, "What shall we do with a queen who dares to disobey the king?"

Memucan, one of the king's wise men answered, "Queen Vashti has wronged not only you, the king, but also every citizen of your empire. Women everywhere will begin to disobey their husbands when they hear about this. Therefore banish Vashti from your presence and choose another queen more worthy than her."

Immediately Ahasuerus followed this advice. But after his wrath had cooled, he began brooding over the loss of Queen Vashti. So his aides suggested, "Let us bring together the most beautiful virgins from your empire. The girl who pleases you most shall be queen instead of Vashti." This advice also pleased the king and he agreed to the plan.

A certain Jew named Mordecai heard of the king's plan. Although Esther was his cousin, he had raised her as his own daughter. Mordecai decided to have Esther enter the contest.

Finally each girl in her turn went in to the king. Many had requested extra trinkets and finery, but not Esther. Her very simplicity only brought out her beauty more than ever. When the king saw Esther, he loved her above all the other virgins. The king set the royal crown upon her head. So Esther the orphan became Esther the queen.

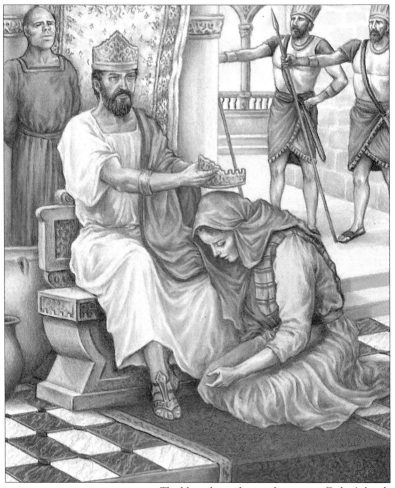

The king places the royal crown on Esther's head.

Parents: *He that followeth after righteousness and mercy
              findeth life, righteousness, and honor.*
              (Proverbs 21:21)

Children: 1. Who was the orphan girl?
              2. What made the king angry?
              3. Why did the king choose Esther?

111

IN THE PALACE OF SHUSHAN
Esther's Great Decision

After Esther had become queen, King Ahasuerus honored Haman, one of his aides and set him above all the princes. He commanded all the palace servants to bow before Haman. But Mordecai the Jew, who worshiped only God, refused to bow to him. Outraged, Haman told the king, "There is a certain race of people scattered throughout your kingdom that refuses to obey the king's laws. If it pleases the king, let a law be made that these Jews be destroyed."

The king agreed to this request, and it was decided that all the Jews would be killed on a certain day. He gave Haman his ring to seal the new law. Soon many copies of it were rushed all over Persia. Then Haman celebrated by drinking wine with the king. But neither the king or Haman knew that Queen Esther was a Jewess.

The Jews were stunned when they heard of the terrible new law. Mordecai mourned openly in the city of Shushan. He told Esther to go and ask the king for mercy, even though she would be risking her life. "Who knows," he said, "if God has brought you into the palace for such a time as this!"

After three days of fasting, Queen Esther, dressed in her royal robes, went to the king. Would he condemn her to death for coming without being called? No, Ahasuerus welcomed her to him. Instead of making known her real request right away, she merely invited the king and Haman to a banquet she had planned.

How honored Haman felt! He boasted about it to his wife Zeresh. "But all this does me no good," he said, "as long as I see Mordecai refusing to bow to me!"

"Well," suggested Zeresh, "prepare a gallows for Mordecai. In the morning ask the king to let you hang him on it."

King Ahasuerus knew that his queen had some special favor to ask. The next day at the banquet he said, "Tell me, what is your wish?" Esther replied, "I only ask for my life and the lives of my people, for we are about to be killed by this wicked Haman."

When the king heard this, he was furious with Haman. One of his servants said, "Haman has planned to hang Mordecai on a seventy- five foot gallows."

"Hang Haman on it," the king thundered. So Haman was hanged on his own gallows.

112

Esther 3 - 8

Esther saves the Jews by revealing Haman's plot.

Parents: *For there is nothing covered, that shall not be revealed; neither hid, that shall not be known.* (Luke 12:2)

Children: 1. Who wanted to destroy all the Jews?
2. Was Esther a Jew?
3. Why was a gallows made?

113

ISAIAH -- CALLED OF GOD
Prophet With a Fervent Zeal

At a time of great trouble in Israel, God raised up Isaiah, one of the greatest prophets who ever lived. He wrote the Book of Isaiah in the Bible. Isaiah has been called the prince of prophets because of his powerful descriptions of God's justice and His plan of redemption. The great prophecies of the coming Messiah, the Lord Jesus, are the crowning of his book. The book of Isaiah is like a miniature Bible.

If we remember that Isaiah lived at a time of wicked rulers, it will help us to understand why he wrote as he did. Notice these words describing Israel: "Ah sinful nation, a people loaded with iniquity, a seed of evil doers, children that are corruptors."

He pronounced a woe, or curse, upon those who were corrupt. Some said evil was good, but good was evil. They called darkness light and called light darkness. Some Israelites mixed strong drinks. They accepted bribes to excuse criminals, but condemned the righteous.

Isaiah also wrote about himself and about the vision he had from heaven. He saw the Lord sitting upon the throne of the universe, dressed in His royal robes. Above Him were heavenly beings with six wings. They were always flying about and saying, "Holy, holy, holy is the Lord."

This vision helped Isaiah to realize anew that God Himself was on the throne! We also need to be reminded again and again that God is still in control of this world. Earthly rulers rise and fall, but God reigns forever.

Having seen God in His holiness, Isaiah cried, "Woe is me! I am undone! I am speechless!" This is what every unbeliever will say when he stands before God's throne on the day of judgment.

Isaiah brought courage and hope to anyone who would obey the Lord. He promised that someday God would raise up a Deliverer. His name would be Wonderful, Counsellor, The Mighty God, The Everlasting Father, The Prince of Peace. He also wrote, "The ransomed of the Lord shall come with songs and everlasting joy. Sorrow and sighing shall flee away."

Isaiah 1, 6, 9

Isaiah has a vision of the Holy One in heaven.

Parents: *Unto thee lift I up mine eyes, O thou that dwellest in the heavens.* (Psalm 123:1)

Children:
1. Was Isaiah a good prophet?
2. Who did Isaiah see seated on the throne?
3. How did Isaiah feel when he saw God's holiness?

GOD CALLS JEREMIAH
Judah's Last Chance

Once again the children of Israel were serving idols. God sent many prophets to them, but they ignored them and would not repent.

Jeremiah was one of God's prophets. Because he had preached against Judah's sin, he was put in prison. He could not go into the house of the Lord. So he sent for Baruch his secretary. Baruch was to write down the message that Jeremiah had received from the Lord. Jeremiah hoped that the people would hear the prophecies, cry to God for mercy, and forsake their sinful ways.

So Baruch wrote God's message on a scroll. He read it in Jerusalem to a crowd who had gathered for a day of fasting. He read about terrible times ahead, when God would punish them for their sins. Jerusalem would be broken down. Their beautiful temple and their houses would be burned. The people would be marched away as slaves to a strange land.

Baruch also read this message of grace, "If you are sorry for your sin and start obeying God, these things will not happen."

The princes of Judah were frightened when they heard God's Word. They said, "The king must hear this message." They told Baruch to hide the prophet while they read the scroll to King Jehoiakim.

So the scroll was read to the king while he sat beside his fire-place. Every time three or four pages had been read, the king cut them out with his penknife and threw them into the fire. The princes begged him not to burn God's Word, but he continued until all of the scroll was destroyed. He was not afraid of all the trouble that was coming. Instead, he was angry with Jeremiah and with Baruch. He sent his servants to seize them, but the Lord had hidden them.

Then the Lord commanded Jeremiah to write another scroll, adding even more curses. King Jehoiakim could burn Jeremiah's scroll, but he could not destroy the Word of God. Likewise, men today can burn the paper, but they will never destroy "The Book"!

Jeremiah 36

King Jehoiakim angrily burns the pages of God's message to His people.

Parents: *And they shall know that I am the Lord, and that I have not said in vain that I would do this evil unto them.* (Ezekiel 6:10)

Children:
1. Who told Jeremiah what to write?
2. How did the king destroy the scroll?
3. Why did the king hate Jeremiah?

FOUR HONEST BOYS
Daniel, Shadrach, Meshach, and Abednego

Because of the sins of Judah, many of the people, called Hebrews, were taken to Babylon as captives. During this time, Nebuchadnezzar the king made a huge statue of gold that looked like a man. Then he called all his princes, rulers, and judges together for a special meeting. Although Daniel did not attend it, his three Hebrew friends, Shadrach, Meshach, and Abednego were there. The large crowd gathered before the statue. Then the king's messenger called out, "When you hear the music, all of you must kneel down and worship the golden image. Anyone who refuses to bow will be thrown into the fiery furnace."

The music was played and everyone knelt -- all but three young men. Shadrach, Meshach, and Abednego stood tall even though their lives were at stake. Immediately some jealous Chaldeans reported them to the king.

Nebuchadnezzar was angry with them. "Is it true," he asked, "that you refuse to worship my golden image? I will give you one more chance, and if you obey, fine. But if you still refuse to worship my image, you will be thrown into the fiery furnace." Then he sneered, "And whose God will deliver you out of my hand?"

The three Hebrew boys had decided long ago what they would do. "We will not worship your image," they answered. "Our God whom we serve is able to deliver us, and He will soon save us, either by life or by death!"

The king's face flushed with rage. "Tie those Hebrews," he roared, "and throw them into the furnace. Make it seven times hotter than ever before!" Immediately his orders were obeyed.

As the king was gazing into the furnace, suddenly he cried out, "I see four men walking in the fire! The fourth one looks like an angel." Then he called, "Shadrach, Meshach, and Abednego, come out!"

Calmly the young men stepped out of the furnace. Nebuchadnezzar and his servants stared at them in amazement. Though the ropes were gone, not one hair was singed or any clothing burned. They did not even smell of smoke.

Then the humbled king gave glory to the God of the Hebrews.

Daniel 3

The Lord saves the three Hebrews from the fiery furnace.

Parents: *Fear not them which kill the body, but are not able to kill the soul: but rather fear him which is able to destroy both soul and body in hell.* (Matthew 10:28)

Children:
1. Can you pronounce Neb- u- chad- nez'- zar?
2. How many men were put into the fiery furnace?
3. How many men did the king see in the furnace?

BELSHAZZAR'S FEAST
Handwriting on the Wall

After Nebuchadnezzar, a new king named Belshazzar ruled in Babylon. One day this king invited a thousand of his princes and nobles for a feast to honor his gods.

King Belshazzar and his guests were feasting, drinking wine, and having fun. Suddenly, they saw that a man's hand was writing on the wall. Every eye was fixed on the mysterious fingers as they wrote words that no one could understand. Then like a fixed display, the hand and the writing remained on the wall.

By now the merry-making had stopped. A death-like silence hung over the banquet hall. Everyone was dumbfounded.

King Belshazzar's face was white, and his knees shook in terror. "Bring the magicians and wise men!" he cried. "Whoever reads these words and tells me what they mean will get a great reward!" The wise men were promptly brought to Belshazzar. But no one could understand the writing, or tell him what it meant.

Then the Queen Mother came to the king. "Don't be frightened or upset," she said. "In your kingdom is a man who was brought captive from Israel by your grandfather. His name is Daniel. The spirit of the holy gods is in him, and he can tell you what the words mean."

So King Belshazzar sent for Daniel. When he arrived, the king said, "I have heard that you can solve all kinds of mysteries. If you can tell the meaning of those words, I will clothe you with purple robes, put a gold chain around your neck, and make you the third ruler of the kingdom."

"Keep your gifts, or give them to someone else," Daniel answered. "Yet I will tell you what the words mean. God hates the pride in your heart. You drank wine from the golden cups taken from His temple in Israel. You also praised the gods of silver, gold, wood, and stone."

The king listened intently as Daniel boldly continued, "Because of this, God has sent this message: *Mene, Mene, Tekel, U-phar- sin*. It means: God has ended your reign. You have failed the test. Your kingdom has been given to the Medes and the Persians."

Daniel's words proved true that very night. The Medes and Persians killed Belshazzar and took his kingdom.

Daniel 5

Daniel interprets the message on the wall.

Parents: *A man's pride shall bring him low: but honor shall uphold the humble in spirit.* (Proverbs 29:23)

Children:
1. Was the king afraid when he saw the hand writing?
2. What kind of cups were they drinking wine from?
3. Who told the king what the writing meant?

DANIEL IN THE LIONS' DEN
God's Greatly Beloved

Babylon was now part of the kingdom of Persia. By this time Daniel was an old man, having served his God for more than eighty years. He had received many special blessings from the Lord.

The Persian king, Darius, respected Daniel and made him chief of all the princes and governors. This made the other princes very jealous. So they searched for some fault in Daniel's life, but found nothing. He was faithful and honest. Finally they decided, "Our only chance is his religion!"

They went to the king and said, "All the rulers have agreed to make a law that for thirty days, no one shall ask anything of any god or man, except from you, O king. If anyone disobeys this law, he shall be thrown into the den of lions." Darius fell for their scheme and signed the decree.

The new law did not change Daniel's devotion to God. Three times each day he knelt before his open window. He prayed and thanked God just as he had done before.

The jealous princes spied on Daniel, then hurried to king Darius. They said, "There is a man who does not obey your law. That fellow Daniel is praying to God three times each day."

Then the king was very sorry that he had signed such a decree, for he loved Daniel. He spent all day trying to find a way to excuse Daniel.

That evening the princes returned to the king. "You signed the law," they reminded him, "and it cannot be changed!" So at last the king ordered that Daniel should be cast into the lions' den.

All that night while the king lay sleepless, the lions watched Daniel and sniffed at him. But not one lion bit him. Early the next morning Darius hurried to the lions' den. He called in anguish, "O Daniel, has your God saved you from the lions?" Then he heard a voice. It was Daniel's!

Daniel said, "My God sent His angel to shut the lions' mouths. I am not hurt at all, for I am innocent of wrong-doing."

The king was overjoyed that Daniel's God had saved him. He ordered that the princes who had accused Daniel should be thrown to the lions. The hungry lions destroyed each one of them.

Daniel 6

God protects Daniel from the lions.

Parents: *Fear thou not; for I am with thee: be not dismayed;
for I am thy God: I will strengthen thee; yea, I will help
thee; yea, I will uphold thee with the right hand of my
righteousness.* (Isaiah 41:10)

Children: 1. How often did Daniel pray each day?
2. Why was Daniel put in the lions' den?
3. Did the lions hurt Daniel?

123

JONAH AND THE BIG FISH
A Message of Repentance for Nineveh

Nineveh was a great city. Within its strong walls were stately temples, glittering palaces, and beautiful gardens. But the people of Nineveh were very wicked.

God spoke to the prophet Jonah. He said, "Go tell the people of Nineveh to repent from their great wickedness." But Jonah didn't want to obey. These people were the enemies of the Israelites.

Jonah decided to ignore God's call. He boarded a ship so he could go far away. But he could never get away from God.

God sent a terrific storm on the sea. This was no ordinary storm for the sailors. Desperately they threw their cargo overboard, calling on their gods for help.

What was Jonah doing? The captain found him below the deck, fast asleep. "What's the matter with you?" he cried. "Call on your God! Perhaps He will hear you and save our lives."

Jonah told the sailors that he had disobeyed God. Because of his disobedience God sent this terrible storm. "Throw me overboard," he said, "and the storm will stop!"

The sailors called on the Lord. They pleaded that He would not blame them for Jonah's death. Then they threw Jonah into the raging sea. Immediately the storm stopped! How the sailors marveled! Right there they decided to serve the living God.

What happened to Jonah? A big fish that the Lord had prepared, swallowed him. From inside the fish Jonah prayed earnestly, promising to obey God. Three days later God caused the fish to vomit Jonah out onto the shore.

Now Jonah was willing to go to Nineveh. He preached all over that great city, crying, "Repent! In forty days Nineveh will be destroyed!"

When the king heard this, he covered himself with rough sackcloth, and sat in ashes. He told all the people to fast and pray to God for mercy. When God saw the people humbling themselves, He changed His mind and did not destroy Nineveh.

Because Jonah obeyed God, many thousands of people in Nineveh heard the good news of God's great mercy.

Jonah 1 - 3

God prepares a big fish to swallow Jonah.

Parents: *Whither shall I go from thy spirit? or whither shall I flee from thy presence?* (Psalm 139:7)

Children:
1. Did God know where Jonah was all the time?
2. Where was Jonah when he prayed so earnestly?
3. Did God love the people of Nineveh?

The New Testament

ZACHARIAS AND ELIZABETH
News From Heaven

Zacharias and Elizabeth were a special couple who lived in Jerusalem. Both of them loved and obeyed God. For many years they had prayed for a child, but God had not granted their request.

Zacharias was a priest in the temple. His job was to burn incense in the Holy Place while the people outside prayed and waited for his blessing.

One day the angel Gabriel came to the temple. When Zacharias saw him standing at the right side of the altar, he was frightened. "Don't be afraid," Gabriel said. "God has heard your prayer. Your wife will have a son, and you shall name him John. You will have great joy when he is born, and others will rejoice with you."

Gabriel continued, "John must never drink wine or strong drink. He will be great in God's sight, for he will have the spirit and power of Elijah. John will cause hard hearts to become soft like those of little children. He will make disobedient minds become wise in true faith." "How can this be?" Zacharias asked doubtfully. "What sign will you give me so that I may know this is true? My wife and I are too old to have children now!"

The angel answered, "My name is Gabriel. I stand before God to obey His commands. Because you have not believed me, you will not be able to talk until the child is born. My words will surely come true at the right time."

Meanwhile, the people outside the temple were waiting for Zacharias. They wondered what was taking him so long. When he finally came out, he could not bless the people. He could not speak at all. But they realized by his actions that he had seen a vision.

After the baby was born, most people thought he would be named after his father. But Zacharias surprised them by writing on a tablet, "His name is John."

Now Zacharias could speak again. Filled with the Holy Spirit, he started prophesying and praising the Lord.

Luke 1

Zacharias and Elizabeth rejoice at the birth of their son.

Parents: *Behold, I will send my messenger, and he shall prepare the way before me.* (Malachi 3:1)

Children: 1. Who was Zacharias?
2. What did the angel tell Zacharias?
3. Why was Zacharias unable to talk?

THE ANGEL GABRIEL VISITS MARY

A Saviour Will Be Born

What is more tiresome than a dark night when you cannot sleep? If you are not feeling well, the night hours pass so slowly. At last you see the first sunbeams of the morning. The birds begin to sing, and everything seems to brighten.

The state of the world before Jesus came was like a long, dark night. Israel's prophets wrote that the people walked in darkness. The wonderful "Son-rise" of God's Son would brighten the dark, sinful world.

For a long time nobody knew just when or where the Saviour would be born. Eve, the first mother, was hoping her son might be the appointed one. Moses declared that God would raise unto the people a prophet like himself. Many years later Isaiah prophesied that a virgin would bear a son. Still later the prophet Micah revealed the very town where the child would be born.

Yet nothing happened. As the years rolled by, the prophecies were gradually forgotten. There was no message from heaven for over four hundred years.

But God knew just the right time to fulfill all the prophecies. He sent the angel Gabriel to the earth with a message for a virgin named Mary.

Gabriel knew the city, the right house, and even the very room where he would find Mary. He entered and said, "Hail, Mary, you are highly favored. The Lord is with you."

Mary was frightened by her heavenly visitor. But Gabriel said, "Don't be afraid, Mary. You are going to have a son. He will be very special. He will be the long-awaited Messiah, whose kingdom will last forever."

"How can such a thing happen to me?" Mary asked in wonder. "I am not yet married." Gabriel answered, "The Holy Spirit will come upon you and God's power will rest on you. That is why your child will be God's own Son. Nothing is too hard for God."

"I really don't understand," said Mary quietly, "but I am God's servant. I am ready to do anything He asks me to do."

Luke 1:26 - 38

The angel Gabriel tells Mary she will have a Son.

Parents: *Behold, a virgin shall conceive, and bear a son, and shall call his name Immanuel.* (Isaiah 7:14)

Children:
1. Who sent the angel to Mary?
2. Was Mary afraid when she saw the angel?
3. What did the angel tell Mary?

131

JESUS IS BORN IN BETHLEHEM
No Room in the Inn

One of the greatest events of all time was about to happen! God chose two special boys to be born. Even their names were chosen in heaven. First John would be born to Zacharias and Elizabeth. He would be called the Prophet of the Highest. Then Jesus would be born to the virgin Mary. He would be called the Son of the Highest.

Before Jesus was born Mary visited her cousin Elizabeth. Then baby John was born and soon Mary returned to her home in Nazareth. There Joseph was waiting, and eagerly looking forward to their wedding day. When Mary said that she would have a baby, Joseph was shocked. He thought that Mary had been unfaithful to him.

So Mary told Joseph about her heavenly visitor. Still he doubted. Had she really seen an angel? Was this baby to be God's Son? Was Mary telling the truth?

Joseph decided to break off the marriage as quietly as possible. He did not want Mary to be shamed and publicly disgraced.

But God knew his thoughts. That very night He sent His angel Gabriel to Joseph in a dream. "Don't be upset," he said, "Mary's baby will be born through God's power and His Spirit. You shall name Him Jesus, for He shall save His people from their sins." How relieved Joseph felt to hear this message. Gladly he took Mary as his wife.

Then came the news from the Roman emperor that all the people would be taxed. Everyone must register at his home town. For Joseph this meant going to Bethlehem. So he took Mary on the tiresome four-day journey to Bethlehem. When they arrived, Mary longed for a soft bed. But alas, the inn at Bethlehem was already full. So they had to stay in a stable.

That night Mary's baby was born. Joseph and Mary gazed with joy at the little child. This was the promised Messiah! Joseph said, "We shall name Him Jesus, just like the angel told me. He is the one God sent to save us."

Mary wrapped baby Jesus in long strips of cloth, then Joseph laid Him in a manger.

Matthew 1:18 - 25;
Luke 2:1 - 7

132

Baby Jesus is born in a stable.

Parents: *Unto us a child is born, unto us a son is given.*
(Isaiah 9:6)

Children: 1. Who told Joseph to name the baby Jesus?
2. In what city was Jesus born?
3. Where did they lay Jesus?

THE SHEPHERDS AND THE WISE MEN

God Speaks Through Angels and a Star

A few hours after Jesus was born, Bethlehem got very quiet. Far away a dog barked. The sleeping town had no idea that a great event had just taken place.

Out on a hillside nearby some shepherds huddled sleepily near their flocks. Suddenly a glorious light shone round about them, and an angel appeared. The shepherds were terrified.

"Don't be afraid, for I am bringing you the most joyful news you could hear," the angel said. "Christ the Saviour is born in a stable in Bethlehem. You will find Him wrapped in long strips of cloth, lying in a manger."

At once the whole countryside lit up with glory as thousands of angels appeared. Their musical voices rose in a chorus of praise. "Glory to God in the highest, and on earth peace, good will to men." Then the angels vanished as suddenly as they had come.

The shepherds hurried across the hills and valleys to Bethlehem. There they found the baby Jesus just as the angel had said. They told Joseph and Mary all about the angels.

Finally the shepherds returned to their flocks. They told the wonderful news to everyone they met. How they praised God!

Hundreds of miles away, some wise men saw a very bright star one night. They decided that this was a sign from God, meaning that a new king had been born. Quickly they loaded their camels and traveled to the land of Israel.

At Jerusalem the wise men asked, "Where is the newborn king of the Jews?" They were told that a king should be born in Bethlehem. That night the bright star moved toward Bethlehem. It led the men right to the house where Jesus was.

How glad the wise men were to find Jesus! They knelt down and worshiped the baby king. Then they gave Him gifts of gold, frankincense, and myrrh. This was God's way of providing for His faithful servants, Joseph and Mary.

Luke 2:8 - 20;
Matthew 2:1 - 12

The sheperds listen to the angel's good news.

Parents: *For God so loved the world, that he gave his only begotten Son, that whosoever believeth in him should not perish, but have everlasting life.* (John 3:16)

Children: 1. Why were the shepherds outside at night?
2. Who told the shepherds that Jesus was born?
3. What guided the wise men to the baby Jesus?

135

THE BOY JESUS AT THE TEMPLE
Lost Among the Teachers

Jesus lived in the town of Nazareth until He was thirty years old. The Bible tells us very little about His boyhood. Do you think He was kind and obedient to His parents? Or did He complain when He had to work hard?

Jesus' mother Mary never forgot what the angel Gabriel had told her. She knew that a knowledge of God's Word would make Jesus strong and wise. So she told Him the history of God's people. He learned of Adam and Eve, of Noah's ark, and of the faithfulness of Abraham, Isaac, and Jacob. He was taught about Moses, to whom God gave the Ten Commandments. He heard the stories of heroes such as Gideon, Joshua, David, Daniel, and Elijah. Jesus loved these stories, just as children still do today.

One spring day, Mary, Joseph, and Jesus went to Jerusalem to attend the yearly Passover feast. Jesus was now twelve years old. At that age a Jewish boy was thought to be a young man instead of a child.

When they arrived at the temple court, Jesus was surprised. He saw merchants selling sheep and doves for the sacrifices, at very high prices. Money changers were arguing. Rich people were noisily dropping money into the offering box, making sure they were noticed. Poor people had to wait to be served just because they were poor. It seemed all this "worship" was only an empty habit. People did not seem to be sorry for their sins.

But when Jesus found some teachers in the temple, His heart was filled with joy. Now He could discuss the Holy Scripture with these wise men.

After seven days, the feast ended. Mary and Joseph headed homeward again. At first they thought Jesus was somewhere in the crowd. But after looking for Him and not finding Him they returned to Jerusalem. After three days they found Him in the temple among the teachers, both asking and answering questions. Mary asked Jesus, "Why have you caused us all this worry?"

Jesus answered, "Don't you know that I must be about my Father's business?" These are His first words that are recorded in the Bible.

Luke 2:39 - 52

136

The boy Jesus discusses Scriptures with the teachers at the temple.

Parents: *In [Christ] are hid all the treasures of wisdom and knowledge.* (Colossians 2:3)

Children: 1. Why did Jesus and His parents go to Jerusalem?
2. What did the merchants sell at the temple?
3. Where was Jesus when His parents found Him?

137

A VOICE FROM HEAVEN

The Baptism of Jesus and His Wilderness Experience

I t was time for Jesus to close His carpenter shop. He put away His tools, never to use them again.

Jesus heard that a preacher named John was baptizing by the Jordan river. He understood that His wonderful ministry of preaching, teaching, and healing was soon to begin. The time had arrived for Gabriel's words to come true.

Jesus headed for the Jordan to find His cousin, also called John the Baptist. There He saw religious leaders, tax collectors, and soldiers among the common people. John was saying, "You must turn from your sins. Don't be greedy and selfish. If you have more food and clothing than you need, share with others. Do your jobs well and without grumbling. This is what God wants from you."

As Jesus came closer, John said, "Look! Here is the Lamb of God who takes away the sin of the world." Then he baptized Jesus. Suddenly the sky opened up, and the Holy Spirit came down on Jesus in the shape of a dove. God's voice came from heaven, saying, "This is my beloved Son, in whom I am well pleased."

Immediately Jesus went into the wilderness among the wild beasts to fast and pray. The angels also came to encourage Him.

After Jesus had not eaten for forty days, Satan came to tempt Him. He wanted Jesus to serve him. "If you are the Son of God," he challenged, "turn these stones to bread!"

Next Satan took Jesus to the highest point of the Temple and said, "Jump off! God promised that He would send His angels to catch you."

Then Satan took Jesus to a very high mountain to see all the kingdoms of the earth. He said, "If you worship me I will give all these to you."

But Satan could not persuade Jesus to turn from God's will and serve him. All three times Jesus defeated Satan by quoting the Word of God.

Matthew 3:13 - 17, 4:1 - 11;
Mark 1:1 - 13;
Luke 3:15 - 23;
John 1:25 - 34

John baptizes Jesus in the Jordan River.

Parents: *[He] was in all points tempted like as we are, yet without sin.* (Hebrews 4:15)

Children:
1. Who said, "This is my beloved Son"?
2. Who tempted Jesus in the wilderness?
3. How did Jesus stop Satan?

JESUS BEGINS HIS MINISTRY
Turning Water Into Wine

J esus knew that it was time to begin His wonderful ministry. His work was to let the world know that God's kingdom had arrived on earth. Though He did not proclaim Himself as the king, He showed God's great love and power in many ways.

Jesus needed men to help Him with this great task. So He chose twelve helpers, most of them fishermen. He called them His disciples.

Jesus never begged but simply invited His disciples to join Him. "Follow me," He said. "I will make you fishers of men."

One of His disciples was a tax collector called Matthew. This man gladly gave up his job in order to follow Jesus. He wanted all his friends to meet this wonderful man. So he invited many guests to a big dinner.

But the Jewish religious leaders were offended at this. They said, "All these guests are bad people. If Jesus is a good man, and He is your master, why does He eat with them?"

Jesus answered, "Do you go to a doctor when you are well? No, only the sick people need a doctor. I have come from God to heal and forgive those who are sick because they have sinned."

One day Jesus and His disciples were invited to a wedding. While Jesus' mother was helping to serve the wedding feast, a problem arose. They ran out of wine for the guests. Mary begged Jesus to do something to help. She felt sorry for the groom and his family.

Pointing to six water jars, Jesus commanded, "Fill the water pots full of water." The servants wondered, "Doesn't He know that we need wine, not water?" But Mary had told them to do whatever Jesus said. So the servants carried in more than 100 gallons of water.

When Jesus told the servants to dip from the jars, they noticed something strange. "Look," they cried. "It isn't water anymore -- it's wine!"

Soon everybody was enjoying the delicious wine. They said, "This wine is even better than the first wine."

This was Jesus' first miracle. It caused His disciples to believe in Him and to trust Him more.

John 1:35- 51; 2:1 - 10 **140**

Jesus turns water into wine at a wedding.

Parents: *The Word was made flesh, and dwelt among us, (and we beheld his glory, the glory as of the only begotten of the Father,) full of grace and truth.* (John 1:14)

Children: 1. How many water jars were there?
2. What did Jesus tell them to do with the jars?
3. Who believed in Jesus?

JESUS AND THE SAMARITAN WOMAN

A Revival in Samaria

The noonday sun beat down on Jesus as He rested by Jacob's well, near the town of Sychar. He was waiting for the disciples who had gone to buy their lunch.

Soon a woman came to draw water from the well. When Jesus asked her for a drink, she was amazed. She could tell that Jesus was a Jew. A Jewish man did not usually speak to a Samaritan -- especially not to a woman! "You mean you want water from *me*, even though I am a Samaritan?" she asked. Who was this strange man?

Jesus replied, "If you knew what a wonderful gift God can give you, and who I am, you would ask me for some living water!" He went on, "People soon become thirsty after drinking from this well. But whoever drinks from the living water that I give, will not become thirsty again. It becomes a well that keeps bubbling into everlasting life."

The woman answered, "Sir, give me that water! Then I'll never be thirsty again, and I won't have to walk out here every day."

Then Jesus began to prick her conscience. He said, "Go home and bring your husband." "But I'm not married," replied the woman.

"I know all about your sinful, unhappy life," Jesus said kindly. "You have been married five times, and you're not even married to the man you live with now!"

The woman was astonished. "Sir," she said, "you must be a prophet. I have many questions. But I know that when Christ the Messiah will come, He will explain everything." Jesus answered, "I am the Messiah."

Immediately the woman raced toward the village, leaving her water pot behind. "Come and see the most wonderful man," she cried. "He must be the Messiah!"

Soon a crowd of curious Samaritans followed the woman back to Jacob's well. "Please stay with us for a few days," they begged. "Tell us more about the good news you have brought."

So Jesus stayed at Sychar for two days, and many people believed on Him.

Jesus speaks to a Samaritan woman at Jacob's well.

Parents: *He that believeth on me, as the scripture hath said, out of his [heart] shall flow rivers of living water.* (John 7:38)

Children:
1. What was the name of the well?
2. What did the woman want from Jesus?
3. Did the people of Sychar believe on Jesus?

143

JESUS STOPS A FUNERAL
A Widow's Son Is Returned to Life

What a warm dry day it was in Judea! Jesus and His disciples had already walked more than twenty miles. Wearily the disciples wondered how much further they would have to travel on this rough road.

The disciples had no way of knowing that they were about to see one of the most touching scenes in history. But Jesus did. He knew that they were needed at the city of Nain.

As Jesus and His disciples trudged along, many people joined them. Women left their housework, and men set aside their tools. Some folks brought sick friends to be healed. Curious children darted in and out of the growing crowd. These people were all drawn to Jesus because of His kindness and love.

Finally Jesus and His followers approached Nain. As they arrived at the city gate, they were met by a funeral procession. Leading the procession were four men carrying the coffin. Next came a woman who was weeping, then followed a crowd of mourners.

Now what would happen? Here was a crowd of happy people, meeting a group of sad people.

When Jesus saw the woman, He felt sorry for her. She was a widow who had just lost her only son. "Don't weep," He said tenderly. Then He walked over and touched the coffin. The pall-bearers stopped short and stared. *Who is this stranger, and what does He think He is doing?*

Jesus looked into the face of the dead boy. "Young man, I say unto you, get up!" He commanded. Immediately the boy opened his eyes, sat up, and began to speak. The astonished bystanders took a few steps back. Several gasps were heard. But Jesus calmly helped the boy to his feet and led him to his mother.

With one voice the people joined the woman in praising the Lord. "A mighty prophet has risen among us!" they exclaimed. "We have seen God's hand at work today!"

News of this miracle spread rapidly throughout Judea and the neighboring countries. More and more people heard about Jesus and His wondrous power.

Luke 7:11 - 17

A widow thanks the Lord for returning her son to life.

Parents: *But though he cause grief, yet will he have compassion according to the multitude of his mercies.* (Lamentations 3:32)

Children: 1. Why did children love to be with Jesus?
2. Did Jesus pity the mother?
3. Does Jesus still pity those who are sad?

145

THE MIRACLE OF THE FISHES
The Reward of Obedience

T he first streaks of dawn lightened the horizon as Peter and his friends rowed toward shore. It had been a poor night for fishing. They had not caught one fish.

After dropping the anchors at the shore, the fishermen washed their nets and prepared for the next night's fishing.

Soon Jesus, along with a crowd of people, came walking toward the fishermen. As He preached at the water's edge, the listeners pressed closer and closer. Jesus saw an empty boat nearby and He stepped into it. He asked Peter to row out a little from the shore so that He could sit in the boat while He was teaching.

What a peaceful scene it was! The morning sunshine was casting shadows over the dewy countryside. Waves lapped at the little boat on the peaceful lake. On the shore was a crowd of men, women, and children, listening intently to every word of the Master.

When Jesus had finished speaking, He said to Peter, "Go out and let your nets down where the water is deeper. You will catch a lot of fish."

Doesn't Jesus know that we don't go fishing in the daytime? thought Peter. *What does He know about fishing?* He said, "Master, we have worked very hard all night and didn't catch anything. But at your word, we will try again."

Soon Peter found out that Jesus knew more about fishing than he had thought. His net began to bulge with so many fish that it started tearing. Quickly Peter called to his partners, "Bring your boat and help me!" They pulled the huge catch onto both boats, so that they were in danger of sinking.

The fishermen were all astonished at the power of God. Peter fell down at Jesus' feet. "Leave me, O Lord," he said. "I am a sinful man and unworthy of all this!"

"Don't be afraid," Jesus comforted him. "From now on you shall catch men."

Luke 5:1 - 11

The disciples bring in their great catch of fish.

Parents: *It is vain for you to rise up early, to sit up late, to eat the bread of sorrows: for so he giveth his beloved sleep.* (Psalm 127:2)

Children: 1. Who told Peter to go and catch fish?
2. Did Peter obey?
3. Did Peter catch any fish?

147

JAIRUS' DAUGHTER

A Father's Love for His Child

One day a troubled father named Jairus pushed through a large crowd beside the sea of Galilee. He found Jesus and fell at His feet. "My twelve-year-old daughter is at the point of death," he cried. "Please come and heal her."

Jesus' heart was touched. Here was Jairus, a ruler of the Jewish synagogue, bowing humbly before Him. How he must love his little daughter!

Jesus turned to follow Jairus home. Then He stopped. "Who touched me?" He asked, looking around.

Jesus' disciples gazed at Him in surprise. "What do you mean?" they responded. "People are pressing against you all the time!"

Then a trembling, frightened woman came forward and fell at Jesus' feet. She explained, "When I saw you I said, 'If I could only touch your clothes, I would be healed!'"

Kindly Jesus told her, "Daughter, your faith has made you well. Go in peace and enjoy your health."

While Jesus was still speaking to her, a messenger arrived. "Your daughter is dead," he told Jairus. "Do not bother the Master anymore." How Jairus' heart sank! But Jesus reassured him, saying, "Don't be afraid. Just keep on believing."

As the little group approached Jairus' house, they heard the clamor of many voices weeping and wailing. Jesus promptly hushed the mourners. "Why do you make such a noise?" He asked. "The little girl is not dead. She's only sleeping."

The mourners stared at Jesus. Several of them whispered together, then burst into mocking laughter. "Go see for yourself," they jeered.

Firmly Jesus commanded the people to leave the house. Only Peter, James, and John were allowed to stay with Him and the sorrowing parents. Then Jesus reverently led the way into the girl's room. He took her hand and said, "Little girl, get up!"

Immediately the girl got up and began to walk. How amazed and overjoyed her parents were! No words could express their heartfelt thanks to Jesus.

Matthew 9:18, 23 - 26;
Mark 5:22 - 24, 35 - 43 **148**

Jesus brings Jairus' daughter back to life.

Parents: *I am the resurrection and the life.* (John 11:25)

Children: 1. How old was Jairus' daughter?
2. What did Jesus tell the people in the house to do?
3. How did Jesus make the little girl well?

BARTIMAEUS CRIES OUT
A Blind Man Receives Sight

Almost every day Bartimaeus groped his way to the city gates. The people of Jericho were used to seeing him sitting there, begging for money.

Bartimaeus could not imagine the beautiful colors of the flowers, or the high palm trees towering above him. He could not see the bright sunshine or the faces of those who loved him. Bartimaeus was blind.

How Bartimaeus longed to see! But there had never been any hope -- until now! Somehow, Bartimaeus had heard about a teacher from Galilee who was healing people from all kinds of diseases. This man, Jesus, could make the lame to walk, the deaf to hear, and the blind to see. Surely He must be the promised Messiah, the son of David. If only Jesus would come to Jericho!

One day Bartimaeus heard muffled noises in the distance. Soon his quick ears told him it was a large crowd of people. "What's going on?" he asked a passerby. The man replied, "Jesus of Nazareth is coming." Bartimaeus' heart leaped. Here was his chance. It was now or never!

He cried out, "Jesus, Son of David, have mercy on me!" But nothing happened. So he cried louder.

"Be quiet, you beggar," someone called. "Stop that yelling."

Bartimaeus panicked. He had to make Jesus hear him! "Jesus, have mercy on me!" he cried. Then he heard a kind voice nearby. The man was saying, "Bring him to me." *This must be Jesus*, thought Bartimaeus.

"What do you want me to do for you?" Jesus asked. "Lord," cried Bartimaeus, "I want to be able to see!"

"Go," answered Jesus, "your faith has made you whole."

Suddenly Bartimaeus could see the whole world around him! But that was nothing compared to seeing the loving face of Jesus. Bartimaeus began following Jesus and telling everyone how wonderful He is.

Mark 10:46 - 52;
Luke 18

Blind Bartimaeus receives his sight.

Parents: *Then the eyes of the blind shall be opened, and the ears of the deaf shall be unstopped.* (Isaiah 35:5)

Children:
1. Why did Bartimaeus beg for money?
2. Was he glad that Jesus came by?
3. What did Jesus do for him?

A CRIPPLED MAN HEALED
Jesus Has Power to Forgive Sin

J esus was now becoming quite well-known because of His teaching and healing ministry. More and more people kept flocking to Him. But often Jesus found a quiet place away from the crowds. There He prayed to His Father for strength.

The Jewish religious leaders, called scribes and Pharisees, also followed Jesus. But they had no faith in Him. They only wanted to find fault with Him because they were jealous.

One day Jesus was teaching a houseful of people. Suddenly they heard noises on the roof. Then they saw a hole in the ceiling. Somebody was tearing off the roof!

More and more pieces of the roof came off, then a large object slowly came down. It was a crippled man on a mat! Four men had used ropes to lower him down to Jesus.

Jesus rejoiced to see their faith in Him. He was pleased that the men would go to so much trouble for their sick friend.

Everyone watched Jesus eagerly. Would He perform a miracle? Even though Jesus had never seen this man before, He knew that there was something the man needed even more than bodily healing. So Jesus said, "Son, rejoice, for your sins are forgiven."

The scribes and Pharisees were outraged at Jesus' words! *How dare He forgive this man*, they thought. *God is the only one who can forgive sin. Who does He think He is?*

Jesus knew what the scribes and Pharisees were thinking. He asked them, "Is it any harder to forgive sins than it is to cure diseases? I will show you that I do have power to forgive sins."

Then Jesus turned to the crippled man. "Get up," He said. "Take your mat and go home."

Immediately the man got up and rolled up his mat. He started walking home, all the while joyfully praising God.

The man's four friends and the people who had seen this miracle also praised God. They were amazed at His great power.

Matthew 9:2 - 8;
Mark 2:2 - 12;
Luke 5:17 - 26

A sick man is brought to Jesus for healing.

Parents: *This is the true God and eternal life.* (1 John 5:20)

Children: 1. Was the man able to walk when he arrived?
2. How did the men get the sick man down to Jesus?
3. What did Jesus do for him?

153

FIVE THOUSAND PEOPLE FED
Five Loaves and Two Fishes

J esus had heard that His friend, John the Baptist, had been put to death in prison. He said to His disciples, "Let us find a quiet place to rest awhile."

But many people were trying to see Jesus and would not leave Him alone. As men, women, and children flocked to Jesus, His heart was touched. "They are like sheep without a shepherd," He said.

Soon the hillside was full of people eagerly drinking in Jesus' words. Hours later the disciples suddenly noticed that the sun was setting. These people were a long way from home. "Send the people away," they told Jesus. "It will soon be dark and they haven't eaten all day."

Jesus suggested, "Why don't you feed the people here?" He turned to Philip and asked, "Where can we buy bread to feed all these people?"

Just then Andrew came. "There's a boy here with some bread and fish," he said. "He will gladly give it to you."

All day long Jesus had known what He would do. With that young boy in mind, He had planned a wonderful miracle.

Then Jesus said to the disciples, "Divide the people in groups of fifties and hundreds." So the people sat on the grass in orderly groups.

Looking up to heaven, Jesus blessed the five loaves and two fishes. Then He broke them into pieces and handed them to the disciples. They, in turn, passed them out to the crowd. All five thousand people ate until they were satisfied.

"Gather up the pieces that are left over so that nothing is wasted," said Jesus. The disciples obeyed, and gathered up twelve baskets full of food! What a miracle, for they had started with only five loaves and two fishes.

Does Jesus still plan such wonderful things today? Does He have His eyes on you? Will you give Him all that you have so that others can be blessed?

Matthew 14:15 - 21;
Mark 6:30 - 44;
Luke 9:10 - 17;
John 6:1 - 14

A young boy gives his bread and fish to Jesus.

Parents: *Seek ye first the kingdom of God, and his righteousness; and all these things shall be added unto you.* (Matthew 6:33)

Children:
1. How many loaves of bread did the boy have?
2. How many fish did he have?
3. Did all the people have enough to eat?

WALKING ON THE WATER
Peter Is Saved From Drowning

After the miracle of the loaves and fishes, some Jews tried to force Jesus to be their king. They thought such a man could give them free bread, get rid of the hated Roman rulers, and even rule the world!

Jesus was indeed a king. But He did not need soldiers with swords to set up His kingdom. Jesus would rule in the hearts of those who loved and obeyed Him.

Then Jesus did what every leader should do when under the pressure of public favor. He slipped away from the crowd into a secret place to pray.

That night while Jesus was praying a fierce storm arose on the lake nearby. Jesus sensed that His disciples were in danger in their boat. So, late at night He went to help them. He walked on the stormy lake as though it were dry land.

When the disciples saw this strange figure coming toward them, they cried out in terror. They thought it was a ghost. But Jesus called out, "Be of good cheer, it is I. Don't be afraid!" Then they all knew it was their Lord.

The disciples could hardly believe their eyes. How could Jesus walk on such wild waves? Suddenly Peter had an idea. He called out, "Lord, if it is really you, ask me to come to you on the water."

"Come!" replied Jesus.

Boldly Peter stepped out of the boat. At first it was wonderful. He was actually walking on the water just like Jesus!

But Peter started looking at the foaming, dark waters. He worried -- *what if a big wave knocks me over?* Peter panicked and he began to sink. "Lord save me!" he cried.

At once Jesus reached down and caught Peter. As soon as the two had entered the boat, the lake became calm. At the same time, the group found themselves at the shore.

How could it be? Only a moment ago, they had all been in the middle of the stormy lake! The astonished disciples humbly fell on their knees. They declared, "Truly you are the Son of God."

Matthew 14:22 - 23;
Mark 6:45;
John 6:15 - 21

Peter cries, "Lord , save me!"

Parents: *Be not afraid, only believe.* (Mark 5:36)

Children: 1. Who walked on the water?
2. Who did the disciples think was walking toward them on the lake?
3. What happened when Peter became scared?

ZACCHAEUS - THE LITTLE MAN

A Tax Collector Becomes a Generous Man

J esus and His disciples were walking to Jerusalem for the Passover feast. By the time they came to the city of Jericho, many people had joined them. How fresh and green Jericho looked to the travelers! They gazed at the fragrant balsam and fruitful date palm trees thriving beside bubbling springs of water.

Tax collectors also liked the town of Jericho. It was a good place to get rich, especially for someone as cunning as their chief, Zacchaeus. But all of Zacchaeus' money could not make him truly happy.

Zacchaeus had heard about Jesus, the wonderful teacher and healer. When Jesus arrived at Jericho, Zacchaeus longed for a glimpse of Him. But he had a problem. He was so short that he could not see over the people's heads.

Zacchaeus did not care what anyone thought of him. He ran ahead of the crowd and climbed a sycamore tree. There he perched on a limb to watch Jesus pass by. But Jesus did not walk past. He stopped and said, "Zacchaeus, hurry and come down. Today I must stay at your house."

Zacchaeus could hardly believe his ears. Was this great teacher really talking to him, a hated tax collector? But something was happening in his heart. Zacchaeus scrambled down the tree faster than he had climbed up. Joyfully he welcomed Jesus to his house.

When the people saw Jesus going with Zacchaeus, they began to criticize Him. They said, "How can He be so friendly with such a crooked thief?"

But that day Zacchaeus became a changed man. Standing before the people, he told Jesus, "I will give half of my belongings to the poor. If I have cheated anyone I will give back to him four times as much money as I took." With these words, Zacchaeus was promising to do even more than the law required to make his wrongs right.

Jesus rejoiced at the change in Zacchaeus. "Today salvation has come to this house," He said. His work was not only healing the sick, the lame, the deaf, and the blind, but also making sinful hearts clean. Jesus said, "I have come to seek and to save those who are lost."

Luke 19:1 - 10

158

Zaccheus climbed a tree so he could see Jesus.

Parents: *Christ Jesus came into the world to save sinners.*
(1 Timothy 1:15)

Children:
1. What was the name of the little man?
2. Why did he climb a tree?
3. Did Zaccheus learn to love Jesus?

STILLING THE STORM
Peace in the Midst of Turmoil

I t had been a long, tiring day for Jesus. He had been healing the sick and teaching the crowd at the lake shore since early morning. Now He longed for a quiet place to rest. So Jesus said to His disciples, "Let us cross the lake to the other side."

But it was not easy to get away from the crowd. Everyone wanted to stay with Jesus just a little longer. Finally He and His disciples were able to set sail for the opposite shore of the lake. Some other boats also set off at the same time. No doubt they carried some people who were determined to follow Jesus wherever He went.

Soon Jesus was fast asleep on a pillow in the back of the boat. The disciples relaxed in the cool breeze as they sailed toward the land of Gadara. They watched the sun sliding beneath the horizon and the first few stars winking into view. It was a pleasant evening to be on the Sea of Galilee. There was no hint of the fierce storms that often engulfed the lake.

Then it happened. Black clouds swept down from the mountainside, turning the gentle breeze into a hurricane. The boat began pitching and tossing helplessly in the raging sea. Again and again huge waves smashed against it, sending great surges of water over the sides.

The disciples frantically baled out the foaming water. But more and more water kept pouring into the boat. Even the seasoned fishermen, Peter, James, and John, started to panic.

At last the disciples began to look for Jesus. To their amazement He was still fast asleep. Quickly they awoke Him, crying, "Master, don't you care if we die?"

Gently Jesus rebuked the disciples, "Why are you so fearful? Where is your faith?"

Then Jesus arose and commanded, "Peace! Be still!" Immediately the wind and rain stopped and the lake became calm again.

The disciples were stunned. They asked, "Who is this man that can make the wind and the water obey Him?" Without a doubt, they knew that Jesus must be the Son of God.

Matthew 8:23 - 27;
Mark 4:35 - 41;
Luke 8:22 - 25

Jesus calms a raging storm.

Parents: *All power is given to me in heaven and in earth.*
(Matthew 28:18)

Children: 1. Were the disciples afraid of the storm?
2. Was Jesus afraid?
3. What happened to the storm?

161

JESUS AND THE LITTLE CHILDREN
Who Is the Greatest in God's Kingdom?

One day some parents brought their little children to see Jesus. Some mothers came with tiny babies in their arms. They wanted the Master to lay His hands on them and bless them. But they could not get His attention right away, for He was busy with the crowd. "Don't bother the Master," the disciples told them. "He is too busy for children."

Jesus noticed the parents and children sadly walking away. He was very displeased with His disciples. "Never turn children away!" He rebuked them. "My kingdom is made up of people who are trustful, loving, humble, and forgiving like children. Always let the children come to me."

The humbled disciples quickly called to the parents, "Come back to Jesus. He wants to meet you."

Then Jesus took the children in His arms one by one. He tenderly laid His hands on them and blessed them.

The disciples looked on in wonder. The Master was giving a lot of attention to these little children. Yet He did not act as if the proud Pharisees were very important at all!

At another time some of the disciples were arguing among themselves. Each one thought he was more important than the others. So they asked Jesus, "Who is the greatest in the kingdom of God?"

Jesus promptly set a child in the middle of their circle. He declared, "Unless you have a change of heart and become like this little child, you will never enter my kingdom. A child does not try to be important and rich or to have great power and fame. He loves his parents, trusting them to take care of him. So whoever is humble, trusting his Heavenly Father like a child, is the greatest in God's kingdom."

Jesus continued, "It would be better to have a stone tied to one's neck and be drowned in the deep sea, than to lead a child away from me into sin."

"Children have angels who watch over them from their place before my Father," said Jesus. "The kingdom of heaven is made of such little ones."

Matthew 18:1 - 6, 10;
Mark 9:33 - 37, 10:13 - 16;
Luke 9:46 - 48, 18:15 - 17

Jesus blesses the little children.

Parents: *Out of the mouth of babes and sucklings hast thou ordained strength.* (Psalm 8:2)

Children:
1. Who said, "Jesus doesn't have time for children"?
2. Did Jesus love all the children?
3. Does Jesus love you?

A MOUNTAINTOP EXPERIENCE
Moses and Elijah Talk With Jesus

One day Jesus told His disciples that He would soon suffer much pain. The chief priests and scribes would treat Him cruelly in Jerusalem and would even kill Him. But on the third day after His burial, He would come back to life.

Jesus also instructed His disciples to be faithful, and never to be ashamed of Him. They should not live selfishly, but do good to everyone. Then Jesus promised that before they died, some of them would see the Son of Man coming in His kingdom.

These teachings were new to the disciples. They could not understand that Jesus had come into the world to suffer and die. Instead, they had been planning to reign with Jesus in an earthly kingdom. Now they felt greatly troubled by His words.

About one week later Jesus took Peter, James, and John up on a high mountain. The tired disciples soon fell asleep. Meanwhile as Jesus was praying, a glorious change came over Him. His face shone like the sun, and His clothes became a dazzling white. Then Moses and Elijah appeared from heaven and talked with Him.

The disciples awoke with a start. What had happened to Jesus? They cowered in terror before the three brilliant beings. Somehow the disciples knew that the two from heaven were Moses and Elijah.

Jesus had planned this glorious meeting both for His three disciples and for all future believers. It was a foretaste of the glory that will be His when He returns to earth. Then all His redeemed saints will be with Him. All those who have died before His return will come back to life, like Moses did. Those who are still alive when He comes will be changed in the twinkling of an eye, like Elijah was.

Soon Moses and Elijah vanished. Then a bright cloud covered Jesus and His disciples. A voice spoke from the cloud saying, "This is my beloved Son, in whom I am well pleased. Hear Him."

Matthew 17:1 - 10;
Mark 9:2 - 13;
Luke 9:28 - 36

Three disciples see Jesus with Moses and Elijah.

Parents: *And this voice which came from heaven we heard, when we were with him in the holy mount.* (2 Peter 1:18)

Children: 1. Who were the three disciples who went with Jesus?
2. How did the face of Jesus become? His clothes?
3. What other two men visited Jesus there on the mountain?

JESUS CLEANSES THE TEMPLE
God's House Is Sacred

At the time of the yearly Passover feast, Jesus went to Jerusalem. Three years earlier when He had attended the Passover feast, He had been very sad by the lack of respect for God's temple. With a braided rope whip, He had driven out the merchants and money-changers. He had unloosed the cattle, sheep, and doves.

Now this year the merchants were all back again, busy as ever. God's holy house looked like a market and smelled like a barnyard. How could anyone worship God in such a place? Jesus knew He must bear witness against this disgrace.

So Jesus again drove out all the merchants and upset the tables of the money-changers. He cleared away the seats of those who had been selling doves. He did not let anyone carry any kind of bowl or pitcher through the temple. Then Jesus explained, "It is written in the Prophets, 'My house shall be called a house of prayer for all nations.' But you have made it a den of thieves!"

The Jewish leaders had made a rule that no lame or blind person could enter the temple. They said that only those with perfect bodies should come before the Lord! They forgot that God looks at the heart of a person more than at his body. So Jesus welcomed the lame and blind people into the temple and healed them all!

Soon the children saw Jesus doing good deeds in the temple. These innocent little ones always loved Jesus. They cried out over and over, "Hosanna to the Son of David," (implying: God help the Messiah). What a day it was! Never before had anything like this happened in the temple. Never would it happen again.

The priests and elders should have rejoiced to see so many happy people. Instead, they were very angry.

Jesus asked them, "Have you never read in the Psalms, 'Out of the mouth of children, even infants, you have perfect praise'?"

Matthew 21:12 - 16;
Mark 11:15 - 18;
Luke 19:45 - 48;
John 2:13 - 16

Jesus chases the corrupt money-changers out of the temple.

Parents: *Give unto the Lord the glory due unto his name: bring an offering, and come before him: worship the Lord in the beauty of holiness.* (1 Chronicles 16:29)

Children: 1. What did Jesus do to the merchants?
2. Who sang the song, "Hosanna to the Son of David"?
3. Were the priests and elders happy?

167

THE GOOD SAMARITAN

Showing Love to Others

One day while Jesus was teaching, a lawyer wanted to test Him. The lawyer asked, "Master, what must I do to live forever in heaven?"

Jesus questioned, "What is written in the law? How does it read?" The lawyer answered, "You must love the Lord your God with all your heart, soul, strength, and mind. You must love your neighbor as yourself."

"You have answered correctly," said Jesus. "Do this and you will live." But the lawyer was not satisfied. He asked, "Who is my neighbor?"

So Jesus decided to teach a lesson with this story:

One day a man was traveling the steep, dangerous road from Jerusalem to Jericho. Suddenly some robbers jumped out from their hiding place. They grabbed him, beat him up, and stole his clothes and money. Then they left him lying by the roadside, naked and dying.

Finally, along came a Jewish priest who served God in the temple at Jerusalem. When he saw the bleeding man, he hurried past on the other side of the road.

Next came a Levite, who also worked at the temple. He walked over for a closer look at the wounded man. But he wanted to keep himself clean for his temple duties, so he kept on going.

At last a Samaritan came along. He pitied this suffering man, even though no Jew had ever been kind to him. Immediately he began to clean the oozing wounds. He poured on some soothing oil and bandaged them. Then he carefully lifted the man onto his donkey. He took him to the nearest inn and took care of him until the next morning.

Before the Samaritan left the inn, he gave the innkeeper two silver coins. "Take care of the man until he is well," he said. "If you have any more expenses, I'll pay you when I return."

Then Jesus looked straight at the lawyer. "Which of the three showed love to the wounded man?" He asked.

"The one who was kind to him," answered the lawyer. Jesus said, "Then go and be like him."

Luke 10:25 - 37

The kind-hearted Samaritan helps a suffering man.

Parents: *My little children, let us not love in word, neither in tongue, but in deed and in truth.* (1 John 3:18)

Children:
1. Who took the man's clothes and money?
2. Did the priest and Levite show any kindness?
3. Did the Samaritan love the hurt man?

169

JESUS TEACHES BY PARABLES

Love and Forgiveness

One day some Pharisees, scribes, and lawyers came to listen to Jesus. They were shocked to see thieves, liars, crooks, and immoral people with Him. "Jesus should not let these sinners mix with the 'respectable' Jews," they complained. "Neither should He eat with them."

Jesus heard their grumbling. He told them, "Imagine that you owned one hundred sheep. One night you notice that one lamb is missing. Would you go to bed thinking that one lost lamb doesn't matter? Of course not," Jesus said. "However tired you would feel, you would search diligently until you found it. Then you would gladly bring it back to the sheepfold. You would invite your neighbor to rejoice with you, because your lost lamb has been found."

Jesus continued, "That is the way God feels about people. There is more joy in heaven over one sinner who humbly comes to God than over ninety-nine people who already obey Him."

Peter also needed to learn about how God deals with people. One day he asked, "Master, how many times should I forgive someone who keeps mistreating me? Is seven times enough?"

"No, Peter," answered Jesus. "Keep on forgiving until seventy times seven. Listen to this parable."

A certain king found out that one of his servants owed him millions of dollars. He commanded that this man, his wife, and his children, should all be sold as slaves. But the servant fell on his knees and begged the king for mercy. So the king pitied the man, and erased the debt from his records.

The servant went outside and found another servant who owed him a few dollars. Grabbing him by the neck, he demanded, "Pay me at once!"

"Please be patient and I'll pay you," the servant begged. But the first servant would not listen. He had the poor man cast into prison.

When the king heard this, he was furious. He told the wicked servant, "I forgave you millions of dollars, yet you refuse to forgive only a few dollars. Because of this you must go to prison until you pay me everything."

"Remember," said Jesus, "God will not forgive you unless you forgive one another with your whole heart."

Matthew 18:7 - 14, 23 - 35;
Luke 15:3 - 7

170

The sheperd joyfully brings back his lost lamb.

Parents: *The Son of man is come to save that which was lost.*
(Matthew 18:11)

Children:
1. Did you ever find something that was lost?
2. Did it make you happy when you found it?
3. Is God pleased when people forgive one another?

171

THE PRODIGAL SON
A Lost Son Is Found Again

Jesus wanted the self-righteous Pharisees to understand that God loves both good and bad people. So He told them this parable:

A certain farmer had two sons. One day the younger son asked his father for his inheritance money. So the father gave to both sons their share of the wealth.

Thrilled with his riches, the younger son rushed off to a far-away country. There he spent his money recklessly on wild parties with lots of friends. But one day he had to face some hard truths: his money was gone. His friends were gone because his money was gone. He was hungry, but a severe famine had made food scarce. Now he was just a poor beggar.

The only job the son could find was feeding a farmer's pigs. He became so hungry that he would have eaten the pig feed if the farmer had given him some.

At last the son came to his senses. He said, "At home my father's servants have plenty to eat, but here I am starving. I will go home to my father and ask him for mercy."

So the son traveled homeward. While he was still a good distance away, his father came running to meet him. The father threw his arms around his dirty, ragged son and kissed him. "Father, I have sinned against heaven and against you," the son confessed brokenly. "I'm not worthy to be called your son, but please make me your servant."

But the father was already calling his servants. "Bring the best robe and put it on him," he ordered. "Put a ring on his finger and sandals on his feet. Kill the best calf and prepare a feast."

When the older son heard about this, he became angry. He would have no part of any welcome-home party for his brother. But his father sought him out, pleading that he would join them.

"It's not fair!" the older son burst out. "I have slaved for you many years, and always obeyed you. Yet you never gave me even a kid to make a feast with my friends. But as soon as this disgraceful son of yours comes home, you kill the best calf!"

The father answered, "Son, it was necessary for us to rejoice. Your brother was dead and is alive again. He was lost and is found."

Luke 15:11 - 32   **172**

The prodigal son is welcomed home.

Parents: *Likewise, I say unto you, there is joy in the presence of the angels of God over one sinner that repenteth.* (Luke 15:10)

Children: 1. Where did the younger son go when he received his inheritance money?
2. What did his father do when he saw him coming home?
3. Did his father forgive him when he saw how sorry he was?

173

JESUS WEEPS
Lazarus Is Raised From the Dead

While Jesus was visiting a place far from Judea, He received this message from His friends Mary and Martha: *Lord, the one you love is very sick.* But He did not hurry back to Judea to help His sick friend. For two days He kept on teaching and healing the people around Him. Then He told His disciples, "Let us go to Judea again."

"But the Jews have been trying to kill you," objected His disciples. "Will you go right back there again?"

Jesus answered, "Does not the day have twelve hours? If we walk in the light we won't stumble." Then He added, "Lazarus is dead. I did not go to heal him because I wanted to show you God's glory so you will believe."

After a long day of walking, Jesus and His disciples were almost at Bethany. By this time, Lazarus had already been in the grave four days.

Martha came out to meet Jesus. "Lord," she cried, "If you had been here, my brother would not have died." Jesus said, "Your brother shall rise again."

"I know that he will rise at the resurrection on the last day," said Martha.

"I am the resurrection and the life," answered Jesus. "Whoever believes in me will live forever after he dies. So he will never really die at all. Do you believe this?"

"Yes, Lord," Martha replied. She called Mary and they all walked to Lazarus' grave. A group of their friends also followed along.

Jesus' heart was touched to see the grieving sisters and their weeping friends. He wept with them even though He knew Lazarus would soon come back to life.

"Take away the stone," Jesus commanded. Before the open grave He prayed, "Thank you, Father, for always hearing my prayers. May everyone who is here believe that you have sent me to give life."

Then Jesus called loudly, "Lazarus, come out!"

The startled crowd heard muffled noises inside the grave. They stared awestruck as Lazarus came out, wrapped in graveclothes from head to foot. It was really true -- Lazarus was alive and well.

That day many of Mary's friends believed in Jesus.

John 11:1 - 44

Jesus raises Lazarus from the dead.

Parents: *The hour is coming in the which all that are in the grave shall hear his voice and shall come forth.* (John 5:28 - 29)

Children:
1. What were the names of Lazarus' two sisters?
2. What did Jesus say after the stone was taken away?
3. Who made Lazarus alive?

JESUS RIDES A DONKEY
Weeping Over Jerusalem

When it was almost time for the Passover, Jesus and His disciples came to the town of Bethany. They went to visit Mary and Martha and their brother Lazarus, whom Jesus had raised from the dead. Everyone enjoyed the special dinner that Martha had prepared. Hardly any of them realized how soon Jesus would leave them.

But Mary somehow sensed that Jesus felt sad. Taking a pound of expensive perfume, she poured it on His feet. Then she wiped His feet with her long hair.

What a comfort this was to Jesus! At least one person had understood a little of how He felt as the time of His death drew near. He told His disciples, "She has anointed me for my burial." This story of Mary's loving action is still being repeated by believers the world over, just as Jesus said it would be.

The next day as Jesus was walking toward Jerusalem, He sent His disciples to a nearby village. They were to borrow a young donkey from a certain place.

The disciples brought the donkey to Jesus. It meekly allowed Him to ride it toward Jerusalem, even though no one had ever ridden it before.

Jesus did this to fulfill an old prophecy. Five hundred years before, Zechariah had said, "Tell Jerusalem her king is coming to her, riding humbly on a donkey's colt!"

People from all over the country had gathered in Jerusalem for the Passover. They flocked to Jesus, cheering and spreading out clothes and palm branches ahead of the donkey. "Blessed is the King of Israel that comes in the name of the Lord! Hosanna! (God save)," they shouted again and again. Many in the crowd were praising Jesus because He had healed them.

All this excitement caused fresh hope to spring up in the disciples. Maybe Jesus would be crowned King now! But why had the donkey stopped?

They gazed at Him in surprise. He was looking toward the city and weeping.

"Oh, Jerusalem," Jesus cried, "eternal peace was within your reach. But you turned it down, and now it's too late." Sadly He continued, "How often I have wanted to gather your children to me as a hen gathers her chickens under her wings, but you would not let me."

Matthew 21:1 - 9;
Mark 11:1 - 10;
Luke 19:29 - 43;
John 12:12 - 19;
Zechariah 9:9

176

The people welcome Jesus to Jerusalem.

Parents: *Lift up your heads, O ye gates; and be ye lifted up, ye everlasting doors; and the King of glory shall come in.* (Psalm 24:7)

Children:
1. Where did Mary put the perfume?
2. On what animal did Jesus ride?
3. Who wept over the people of Jerusalem?

177

THE LAST SUPPER
Loving Last Words

J esus wanted a quiet, safe place to enjoy His last Passover feast with the disciples. He told Peter and John, "Go into Jerusalem and look for a man carrying a pitcher of water. Follow him to his house and he will show you a large room upstairs. There you may prepare our Passover meal."

Meanwhile Judas, one of the disciples, had secretly gone to the chief priests. He asked them, "How much money will you give me if I help you catch Jesus?" The chief priests were delighted to hear this from one of Jesus' own followers. They promised to give Judas thirty silver coins.

Soon the Passover feast was ready, and they all sat down at the table. "I have been looking forward to this hour with deep longing," said Jesus. "I want to eat this Passover meal with you once more before I suffer."

Although Jesus loved to be with the disciples, His heart was heavy that evening. During the meal He said, "One of you is going to betray me to my enemies!" Shocked and grieved, the disciples looked at each other. One by one they asked Jesus, "Am I the one?" Jesus answered, "It is the one to whom I give this bread after I have dipped it in the sauce." As He spoke He gave it to Judas Iscariot. Jesus told him, "Do quickly what you are going to do."

Then Judas went out into the night as dark as his heart. He could hardly wait to get his hands on all those shining coins. That evening Jesus changed the old Jewish Passover into the new Lord's Supper. First He broke a loaf of bread and handed the pieces to His disciples. "Eat this bread, for it stands for my body," He said.

Next Jesus took a cup of wine. He said, "Drink this wine, because it stands for my life-blood which will be shed for the sins of many. Keep on doing this again and again to remember me. I will not drink wine again until the day I drink it with you in my Father's kingdom."

As the farewell supper ended, the disciples sang a hymn with their Lord Jesus for the last time.

Matthew 26:17 - 30;
Mark 14:12 - 26;
Luke 22:7 - 23;
John 13:21 - 30

Jesus eats his last Passover meal with His disciples.

Parents: *Christ our passover is sacrificed for us.*
(1 Corinthians 5:7)

Children: 1. How many silver coins did Judas get?
2. What did they eat at the Lord's supper?
3. What did they drink?

MANSIONS IN HEAVEN
Farewell Prayer of Jesus

After the last supper, Jesus talked to His disciples for a long time. He wanted to prepare them for the difficult days ahead. "You must trust and believe in me, just as you believe in God," He said. "I am going to leave you soon. But after I have risen from the dead, we shall meet again in Galilee. Do not be overcome by fear or despair, even when it seems as though everything has gone wrong."

Jesus continued, "When I return to my Father, I promise not to leave you alone. My Father will send the Holy Spirit to comfort you. Although you will not be able to see Him, He will guide you in the true way. He will help you to remember the things that I have taught you. He will also give you courage when you find it hard to obey my commandments."

"I will prepare beautiful mansions for you in heaven," said Jesus. "Then one day I will come again to take you home. You already know the way to heaven."

But Thomas said, "Lord, we have no idea where you are going. How can we know the way?" "I am the way to God," answered Jesus. "I am the only bridge from earth to heaven. No one can come to God except across that bridge."

Jesus said lovingly, "Before I leave you, I will give you the gift of peace -- *My Peace*. It is not the world's kind of peace. My peace will keep you strong and joyful even during hard times."

Then Jesus prayed a most beautiful prayer. Lifting His eyes to heaven, He said, "Holy Father, I have told these disciples all about you. Keep them safe from Satan's power. Make them pure and holy through your truth. I pray not only for these with me, but also for all those who will believe in me from this time until the end of the world."

After Jesus finished talking to His disciples, they went out into the night. They crossed the brook Kidron and entered the garden of Gethsemane. There Jesus prayed in anguish but His disciples fell asleep.

John 14 - 17

Jesus prays earnestly in the garden while His disciples sleep.

Parents: *Surely He hath borne our griefs and carried our sorrows.* (Isaiah 53:4)

Children: 1. Where did Jesus say He was going?
2. Where is Jesus now?
3. What is Jesus preparing for those who love Him?

A NIGHT IN GETHSEMANE

A Kiss of Betrayal

J esus and His disciples came to the Garden of Gethsemane. They were all very tired. "Please stay close to me," He said to Peter, James, and John. "My heart is very heavy."

Then Jesus took a few steps further and fell to the ground. He was almost overwhelmed with grief. "My Father," He prayed earnestly, "Would it be possible for you to take away this terrible suffering that I face? Yet I will accept whatever you want for me."

Just then an angel came from heaven to strengthen Jesus. He was in such agony that bloody sweat was dripping from His face.

At this time when Jesus needed His disciples the most, they were fast asleep. Twice Jesus woke them, but they soon dozed off again. "Couldn't you stay awake with me for even one hour?" Jesus asked them. "But now you must get up. A mob is coming to arrest me!"

Suddenly the disciples heard the clattering of metal and the thudding of many marching feet. They saw swords glinting in the light of flickering lanterns and torches. The band of Jewish priests, soldiers, and elders was coming right toward them. To the disciples' horror they saw that Judas was leading the mob!

Judas walked up to Jesus and kissed Him. What a mockery of friendship! But Jesus calmly asked, "Do you betray the Son of Man with a kiss?"

Then Jesus asked the mob, "Who are you looking for?" "Jesus of Nazareth," they exclaimed. Jesus answered, "I am He." As He spoke they all fell backwards to the ground. Yet Jesus did not try to get away. He only asked them not to arrest His disciples.

"Shall we use the sword?" the disciples asked. Swiftly Peter's sword flashed out, cutting off the right ear of the high priest's servant.

"Put away your sword," said Jesus. "Those who use the sword will die by the sword." Then He gently put the ear back in place and healed it. In this last miracle before He suffered for all mankind, He showed His love for His enemies.

Matthew 26:36 - 52;
Mark 14:32 - 43;
Luke 22:39 - 51;
John 18:1 - 11

Judas betrays Jesus with a kiss.

Parents: *Yea, mine own familiar friend, in whom I trusted, which did eat of my bread, hath lifted up his heel against me.* (Psalm 41:9)

Children:
1. Who kissed Jesus in the garden?
2. Who cut off the servant's ear?
3. Who healed the ear?

JESUS IS CONDEMNED
Trial by False Witnesses

T he plot to capture Jesus had been successful. Yet Judas felt more and more miserable. How could he have been so wicked? He went back to the temple to see the priests. "I am guilty of betraying an innocent man," he confessed. "That's your problem," they replied coldly.

With a cry of despair Judas flung the thirty silver coins across the floor. Then he went out and hanged himself.

Meanwhile, the mob had brought Jesus before the two Jewish leaders, Annas and Caiaphas. He stood alone and friendless, surrounded by accusing priests and Pharisees. How they hated Him! Somehow He always made their proud, make-believe goodness look so cheap and unclean. Now they could finally get rid of Him.

Though Jesus was very tired, the men did not let Him rest. They spit in His face. They blindfolded Him, then struck His head with their fists. "Tell us who hit you!" they jeered.

During this time Peter had been warming himself at a fire nearby. First one bystander, then another declared that Peter was a follower of Jesus. Both times Peter denied it. The third time he was accused, Peter became angry. Cursing and swearing, he shouted, "I don't even know the man!"

Just then a rooster crowed, and Jesus looked straight at Peter. In a flash, Peter remembered that Jesus had said, "Before the rooster crows two times you will deny me three times." Peter felt terrible! Overcome with remorse, he went out and wept bitterly.

As a new day dawned, the whole Jewish council took Jesus to the court of Pilate the governor. "This man is a trouble-maker," they accused. "He tells the people not to pay taxes to the Roman government. He even claims to be a king!" More voices chimed in, shouting all kinds of slander.

Pilate could soon tell that the Jews had brought Jesus because they were jealous of Him. He questioned Jesus carefully, but found Him innocent of any crime. In fact Jesus seemed far more honorable than the Jewish council.

But what could Pilate do? The crowd was becoming louder and wilder every minute. "Crucify Him!" they roared. "Put Him to death!"

Matthew 26:27 - 27:32;
Mark 14:53 - 15:21;
Luke 22:63 - 23:26;
John 18:19 - 19:15

Jesus is on trial before Pilate the governor.

Parents: *Godly sorrow worketh repentance to salvation...but the sorrow of the world worketh death.*
(2 Corinthians 7:10)

Children:
1. What did the rooster do early in the morning?
2. What was the governor's name?
3. What did the mob say should be done with Jesus?

185

JESUS IS CRUCIFIED
Greatest Day That Ever Was

Pilate did not know what to do. He did not want to condemn an innocent man. Besides, his own wife had sent him this message: *Leave that righteous man alone. This morning I have suffered much pain in a dream because of Him.*

But the blood-thirsty mob kept roaring, "Crucify Him! Crucify Him!" Soon they all began to shout, "Set Barabbas free!" These Jews did not really care about Barabbas, who was a convicted criminal. But they knew that Pilate usually freed one prisoner during this time. They would free anyone else, even a murderer, rather than Jesus.

Nervously Pilate washed his hands before the crowd. He said, "I am not responsible for this man's death." Yet he tried once more to save Jesus. He ordered his soldiers to whip Him severely. Then they forced a crown of thorns on His head, dressed Him in a purple robe, and placed a stick (a mock scepter) in His right hand. Surely now the Jews would pity Jesus when they saw His bloody face and clothes. Pilate brought Him before them and said, "Behold the man!"

But the mob only became louder. "Away with Him! Crucify Him!"

At last Pilate gave up. He allowed them to take Jesus out of the city to a place called Golgotha. There He was nailed to a cross.

Though Jesus was in agony, He did not hate His enemies. He prayed, "Father forgive them for they do not know what they are doing."

Two thieves were also crucified that day, one on either side of Jesus. One of them taunted, "If you are Christ, save yourself and us also!" But the other thief said, "We deserve to die, but this man is innocent." Turning to Jesus he pleaded, "When you come into your kingdom, remember me."

Immediately Jesus answered, "You will be with me in paradise this very day!"

At noon the whole world was plunged into darkness. Jesus kept on suffering for three more lonely hours. Just before He died, He gave a shout of victory. "It is finished!" His work on earth was done. Now He could free the whole world from the grip of sin and Satan.

Suddenly the earth shook, rocks split apart, and many graves were opened. The frightened soldiers exclaimed, "Surely this was the Son of God!"

Matthew 27:29 - 44;
Mark 15:16 - 28;
Luke 23:26 - 43;
John 19:17 - 29

Jesus is crucified between two thieves.

Parents: *The blood of Jesus Christ his Son cleanseth us from all sin.* (1 John 1:7)

Children:
1. Where was Jesus' cross placed?
2. How many men were crucified?
3. Why did Jesus die?

JESUS IS RISEN!

A Glorious Morning

Jesus' faithful friends had been watching the crucifixion from a distance. In helpless misery they had listened hour after hour to His cries. It had been heart-breaking to watch their beloved Master die! Surely this day, as God's wrath against sin was poured on His own perfect Son, had been the harshest hour in human history.

Could it be that only this week Jesus had triumphantly ridden into Jerusalem before cheering crowds? Now within twenty-four hours, He had been betrayed, tried, condemned, and crucified. What was there to live for now?

Late on the afternoon of the crucifixion two honorable men named Joseph and Nicodemus came to the cross. They had not been following Jesus openly because they were afraid of the Jewish leaders. These men who loved Jesus, pulled out the nails that had been driven into His hands and feet by men who hated Him. They wrapped His body in linens fragrant with sweet spices. Then they buried Him in a new tomb.

The next day some priests and Pharisees went to Pilate. They said, "This deceiver once said that in three days He would rise again. Now issue an order to have the tomb guarded. Otherwise His disciples may come and steal the body, claiming that He arose from the dead. That would be the worst deception of all!" So Pilate commanded that the tomb must be guarded day and night.

Very early the next morning a great earthquake shook the tomb. A blinding light flashed on the sleepy soldiers standing guard. It was an angel from heaven, with a face like lightning and a robe as white as snow. The terror-stricken guards shook like a leaf before him, completely helpless. The angel rolled the huge stone away from the entrance and sat on it. Then in power and great glory Jesus rose from the dead and vanished into the night.

Meanwhile three women named Salome, Mary Magdalene, and another Mary were coming toward the tomb. They were frightened when they saw the angel. But he said kindly, "Do not fear. I know you are looking for Jesus which was crucified. He is not here, for He is risen! Go quickly and tell His disciples."

The women fled from the tomb, trembling and speechless. Their hearts were filled with both fear and great joy.

Matthew 27:55 - 28:1 - 10;
Mark 16:1 - 14;
Luke 24:1 - 49;
John 20:1 - 23

The women worship Jesus after His resurrection.

Parents: *He was declared to be the Son of God with power, according to the spirit of holiness, by the resurrection from the dead.* (Romans 1:4)

Children: 1. Who guarded the tomb?
2. Who rolled away the stone?
3. What did the angel say to the women?

DOUBTING THOMAS
The Virtue of Believing Without Seeing

Mary, Salome, and Mary Magdalene ran to find Peter and John. They exclaimed, "When we came to the tomb, an angel was there. He said that Jesus is risen!"

Could it really be true? Immediately Peter and John both ran toward the tomb, but John arrived first. He stooped down and looked inside. Then Peter came running up behind him and promptly entered the tomb. They noticed that all the grave clothes still lay neatly in place. Surely the grave clothes would also be gone if the body had simply been stolen. They left the tomb shaking their heads.

Mary Magdalene walked back to the tomb. Through her tears, she noticed two angels sitting inside the tomb.

"Why do you weep?" asked the angels. Mary sobbed, "I don't know where my Lord is."

Turning around, Mary saw Jesus standing nearby, but she thought He was the gardener. "Why are you weeping?" Jesus asked. Mary replied, "Sir, tell me where you have laid Him."

Then Jesus said, "Mary!" At once she knew Him. "Rabboni -- Master!" she cried joyfully.

That evening the disciples met behind locked doors, because they were afraid of the Jews. Suddenly Jesus appeared before them. He said, "Peace be to you." How glad they were to see their Lord.

But one disciple, Thomas, was missing that evening. When they saw him, they exclaimed, "We have seen the Lord! He is risen from the dead!"

"I wonder," said Thomas doubtfully. "Unless I see the nail prints in His hands, and feel the wound in His side, I will not believe."

A week later the disciples met again. This time Thomas was with them. All at once they looked up, and there stood Jesus.

As before, Jesus said, "Peace be with you." He looked straight at Thomas, and said, "Put your fingers here and look at my hands. Put your hand in my side. Do not doubt, but believe."

In stunned surprise, Thomas could only confess, "My Lord and my God!" "You believe because you have seen me," said Jesus kindly. "Blessed are those who believe even though they have not seen me."

John 20:1 - 31

Jesus shows Thomas His nail prints.

Parents: *Let us hold fast the profession of our faith without wavering (for he is faithful that promised).* (Hebrews 10:23)

Children: 1. What two men ran to the tomb?
2. Who did Mary see in the garden?
3. Which disciple did not believe?

191

ON THE ROAD TO EMMAUS
Becoming Aware of Christ's Presence

Two of Jesus' followers were walking the seven miles from Jerusalem to their home in Emmaus. They felt sad and confused. What had happened to Jesus? Some people claimed that His body had been stolen from the tomb. Some women were spreading a strange story about angels who said Jesus was alive. Other people declared that saints who had been buried long ago were walking the streets of Jerusalem.

As the two men were talking, Jesus joined them, but they didn't recognize Him. "What are you discussing that makes you so sad?" Jesus asked.

"You mean you haven't heard?" Cleopas exclaimed. "You must be a stranger in this area. Our Master Jesus was a mighty prophet, but He was put to death. We were certain that He was the one who would redeem Israel. But now our hopes are gone!" He went on to relate the unusual happenings of the last few days.

Then Jesus replied, "How foolish and slow you have been to believe! Don't you know that the prophets wrote about the Messiah? It was necessary for Him to die, but not for any crime that He committed. He died for the sins of all people in order to bring them peace and forgiveness."

Then Jesus taught them a glorious Bible lesson from Genesis to Malachi. He explained that the Messiah was to suffer, die, and rise from the dead before He would be their king.

By this time the three had arrived at Emmaus. Showing hospitality, Cleopas invited the visitor for supper. While Jesus was asking God's blessing on the food, the two disciples suddenly knew who He was. At that moment He vanished out of their sight.

Forgetting that they were hungry and weary, Cleopas and his friend headed straight back to Jerusalem. "No wonder our hearts grew warm when He talked to us!" they exclaimed. In Jerusalem they found the eleven disciples talking excitedly.

"Jesus is risen!" the disciples declared. As they were talking, Jesus once again appeared before them. "Peace be unto you," He said comfortingly. How the disciples rejoiced to see their Lord once more!

Luke 24:13- 49;
Mark 16:12- 13

192

Jesus explains the Scriptures to Cleopas and his friend.

Parents: *If Christ be not raised, your faith is vain, ye are yet in your sins.* (1 Corinthians 15:17)

Children:
1. Why were Cleopas and his friend sad?
2. Who joined them as they were walking to Emmaus?
3. Who died so that we might have peace and forgiveness?

193

THE GREAT COMMISSION
Proclaiming the Good News

Now it was time for the disciples to leave Jerusalem and go to Galilee. The angels at the tomb had said that Jesus would meet them there. But some disciples still did not believe that Jesus had risen from the dead. When Jesus appeared He reproved them for their stubbornness and unbelief.

Then Jesus opened their minds so they could understand the Scripture. "Remember what I used to tell you?" He asked. "I said that everything written about me must happen -- everything in the law of Moses, the Psalms, and the Prophets. These writers foretold that Christ would suffer, die, and rise from the dead on the third day. They wrote that men's hearts would be changed and their sins forgiven by the power of my name."

"Now you must go everywhere and tell the good news of salvation to all people," Jesus continued. "Anyone who believes and is baptized shall be saved, but anyone who does not believe will be condemned. You must teach believers to observe all that I have commanded you. Remember, I will always be with you, even to the end of the world. As my Father sent me, so I am sending you."

"Those who believe will be able to perform miracles in my name," said Jesus. "They will drive out evil spirits and speak in foreign languages. If they are bitten by snakes or if they drink deadly poison, it will not hurt them. They will lay their hands on the sick to heal them. I promise to protect all those who truly believe in me."

Finally Jesus breathed on the disciples and said, "Receive the Holy Spirit." In this same way, God had breathed the breath of life into the first man Adam to make him a living soul. By this spiritual breath of life, Jesus was preparing the disciples for a great work. He wanted them to spread the good news about salvation after He had returned to heaven. There, even now, He is preparing an eternal home for every one who loves and obeys Him.

Matthew 28:16 - 20;
Mark 16:14 - 18;
Luke 24:44 - 49

Jesus tells His disciples to take the Good News to all the people.

Parents: *Blessed are they that have not seen, and yet have believed.* (John 20:29)

Children:
1. To whom should the disciples tell the good news of salvation?
2. Did Jesus promise to always be with His disciples?
3. Does Jesus still care for His people?

JESUS' LAST VISIT AND ASCENSION

Forty Wonderful Days

During the forty days after Jesus had risen from the dead, He appeared to His friends at many different times. But He showed Himself only to those who believed on Him. The ones who hated Him would never again see the Saviour of the world here on earth.

By this time there was no longer any doubt that Jesus was alive. Although He could pass through closed doors and disappear instantly, He certainly was not a ghost. His friends could touch Him. He ate fish and bread with the fishermen along the seashore. One time He came to a group of more than five hundred believers who were gathered on a mountainside.

Today there are three special days on calendars all over the world: Christmas, Good Friday, and Easter. These days stand for the birth, death, and resurrection of Jesus.

At the time of the crucifixion, God seemed to withhold His power. He did not rescue Jesus from a horribly painful death. The disciples were still weak and afraid of the Jews. But during the forty days after His resurrection, Jesus helped them to understand many new things. They received strength to overcome their fear of man. They became strong and bold by the power of God's love, not by fighting earthly battles.

One day Jesus was teaching His disciples on the Mount of Olives near Bethany. "I will soon go home to my Father in heaven," He said. "You will not see me anymore. But you shall be my witnesses, first in Jerusalem, and then throughout the whole world. Teach the people to follow me."

"Stay in Jerusalem until I send the Holy Spirit," Jesus continued. "He will guide you in the right way, and provide strength, wisdom, and courage."

Then Jesus lifted up His hands to bless His disciples. Suddenly they saw that He was rising! Higher and higher He went until He disappeared in a cloud.

The disciples watched in silent wonder. How they wished that Jesus could always stay with them on earth.

Just then two men in shining white clothes stood before them. "Why are you looking up into heaven?" they asked. "This same Jesus will come back some day in the same way you saw Him go."

Then the disciples joyfully went to Jerusalem. Each day they praised God and worshiped in the temple while they waited for the Holy Spirit to come.

Matthew 28:16 - 20;
Mark 16:15 - 18;
Luke 24:49 - 53;
Acts 1:8 - 11

The disciples watch Jesus ascend to heaven.

Parents: *And if I go and prepare a place for you, I will come again, and receive you unto myself; that where I am, there ye may be also.* (John 14:3)

Children:
1. As Jesus spoke to the disciples, where did He begin to go?
2. What did they see Him go into?
3. Where is Jesus now? Is He coming again?

THE DAY OF PENTECOST
God Sends the Holy Spirit

Now Jesus was at home in heaven. His disciples had plainly seen Him ascend up into the sky and disappear in a cloud.

Although the disciples had been sad when Jesus left, they did not despair. They thought about His last instructions. "Go back to Jerusalem and wait there for the Holy Spirit," He had said. "He will give you the power to be my witnesses."

This was all so new to the disciples. How would they receive power? Who was the Holy Spirit? But they still obeyed Jesus' command even though they did not understand at all.

In Jerusalem one hundred and twenty believers gathered in a house. There they stayed for ten days praying and worshiping in beautiful oneness of heart. Eagerly they waited for the Holy Spirit to come which Jesus had promised.

Suddenly they heard a mighty roar like hurricane winds filling the house. They saw something like small forked tongues of fire coming down and sitting on each one of them. But this fire did not hurt them. Instead, they were filled with the Holy Spirit from heaven, just as Jesus had said! Through the Spirit, they received a special ability.

What was this special ability? God soon displayed it powerfully through the disciples. Before this, they had been weak and fearful. But now they could not keep quiet about their Lord. In the temple they found great crowds of worshipers who had traveled from more than eighteen cities and countries.

The people listened intently to the disciples. They were amazed, for everyone could hear them in his own language. It was a miracle! The disciples were speaking languages they had never learned! Many people praised God for His great power.

That day Peter showed how much the Spirit had changed him. Only weeks before he had denied Jesus, but now he was a bold, fearless preacher. His message of Jesus' saving grace was so touching and powerful that three thousand people repented and became believers.

In this way, the Christian church was born by the power of the Holy Spirit.

Acts 1:8 - 14, 2:1 - 36

God sends the Holy Spirit upon the disciples.

Parents: *And it shall come to pass afterward, that I will pour out my spirit upon all flesh.* (Joel 2:28)

Children: 1. Which disciple preached a powerful message?
2. How many people became believers this day?
3. Does the Holy Spirit still help people today?

STEPHEN -- THE FIRST MARTYR

A Glowing Witness

After the disciples had received the Holy Spirit, they preached the gospel of Jesus boldly to many people. More and more people in Jerusalem became believers.

One outstanding preacher was Stephen. Although he was just newly ordained, he preached with great power. "The Gospel of Christ is not only for the Jews," he declared, "but for all those who believe in Jesus Christ." Stephen was willing to accept non-Jewish people called Gentiles as believers, even though many of the Jews despised them.

When some Jews tried to argue with Stephen, they could not resist his wisdom. He gave convincing proof that Jesus was indeed the Messiah. But this only made them angry because they hated Jesus. So they stirred up the people against him. They seized him and brought him before the Jewish council.

"This man never stops speaking evil against this holy temple and the law of Moses," they accused. "We also heard him say that Jesus of Nazareth will destroy this place, and will change the customs which the prophet Moses handed down to us." Of course this was not true. They were twisting his words just like they had done to Jesus. In fact it happened at the very same place.

Then the whole council stared at Stephen for his face was like that of an angel. He was glowing with Christ-like love for his enemies.

The high priest asked, "Are these charges true?"

Stephen began telling the history of the Jews. "Down through the ages the Jewish nation has refused to listen to the leaders that God sent to them," he declared. "And now you have rejected and murdered the greatest messenger of all, God's Son Jesus Christ!" Stung to the quick, the Jews began grinding their teeth at him in anger.

Then Stephen, filled with the Holy Spirit, looked heavenward and said, "Look! I see heaven open, and the Son of Man standing at God's right hand."

The Jews flew into a rage and stopped their ears. Shouting at the top of their lungs, they dragged him outside the city to stone him.

The sharp stones struck Stephen, slashing and battering his body. But falling on his knees he cried out, "Lord, forgive them for this sin." With these words Stephen died.

Acts 6 - 7

The Jewish mob stones Stephen.

Parents: *These are they which came out of great tribulation, and have washed their robes, and made them white in the blood of the Lamb.* (Revelation 7:14)

Children:
1. Why did the Jews throw stones at Stephen?
2. Was Stephen angry at the Jews?
3. Did Stephen pray for them?

PHILIP AND THE ETHIOPIAN
The Response of a Hungry Heart

Immediately after Stephen was stoned, all Christians were hunted like criminals. The attack was led by a devout Pharisee named Saul. Saul thought he was pleasing God by getting rid of those deceivers. Under his direction, men and women of all ages were thrown into prison. Many Christians fled from Jerusalem and were scattered far and wide.

During this time, one of Stephen's fellow-ministers named Philip traveled to Samaria. There he preached to large crowds. In the name of Jesus he healed many paralyzed and crippled people. There was great rejoicing in the city.

In the same city was another man named Simon. For a long time he had enjoyed dazzling the people with his magic charms. They claimed he was the great power of God. But through Philip's ministry, both Simon and many of his followers became believers.

Simon saw the power of the Holy Spirit in Philip, and in Peter, who was helping Philip. He offered money for this power.

But Peter declared, "Your silver perish with you, for no money can buy the gift of God! Your heart is not right with God. You must repent from this wickedness."

Then the angel of the Lord told Philip to leave the busy city and go south on a desert road. There he was led to a man in a chariot. The man was an Ethiopian, the chief treasurer of the queen's court. Somehow this man had heard about the true God, so he had traveled to Jerusalem to worship Him. Now in his long journey home, he was reading the scripture in Isaiah.

"Do you understand what you are reading?" asked Philip as he came near.

The Ethiopian replied, "How can I, unless someone teaches me?" He had been reading about God's servant who was led to die, like an innocent lamb to the slaughter.

Then Philip told him all about Jesus, the Lamb of God, who died for the sins of the whole world.

"See, here is water," said the Ethiopian. "What hinders me from being baptized?"

"If you believe with all your heart, you may," answered Philip. So he baptized him, and the Ethiopian went on his way rejoicing.

Acts 8:4 - 40   **202**

Philip explains the Scriptures to the Ethiopian.

Parents: *For the scripture says, whosoever believeth on him shall not be ashamed.* (Romans 10:11)

Children: 1. Where did the angel tell Philip to go?
2. What was the Ethiopian riding in?
3. What book of the Bible was he reading from?

THE CONVERSION OF SAUL

A Chosen Vessel for God

Saul was a bright young Jew from the city of Tarsus. He was every inch the proud Pharisee, having studied under the famous Jewish teacher, Gamaliel, in Jerusalem. When Saul did something, he did it right.

Saul was present at the stoning of Stephen. He was convinced that this new teaching about Jesus was a false doctrine. So he did his best to wipe out the church in Jerusalem. Next he decided to attack the believers who had scattered to the surrounding areas. He would arrest them, tie them up, and haul them back to Jerusalem for trial.

Armed with official papers from the high priest, Saul gathered his henchmen together. Then they started the eight-day journey to Damascus, the capital of Syria. As they neared the city, suddenly a blinding light, brighter than the noonday sun, shone on them. The light was so brilliant that Saul fell to the ground, totally blind. He heard a divine voice saying, "Saul, Saul, why do you persecute me?"

Saul faltered, "Who are you Lord?"

"I am Jesus," came the reply. "Every time you hurt one of my followers, you are hurting me!"

Then Saul, trembling and astonished, asked, "What will you have me to do, Lord?"

"Go into the city," said the Lord. "There you will be told what to do."

So Saul was led to the house of Judas. For three days he did not eat or drink, but prayed earnestly for the Lord's guidance. In a special vision the Lord showed him that a man would come to help him.

Meanwhile, a disciple named Ananias also saw the Lord in a vision. The Lord told him to meet Saul in Judas' house and lay hands on him. Ananias did not really want to go, because he knew how much Saul had been persecuting the believers. But he trusted the Lord and went anyway. As Ananias laid his hands on Saul, he said, "Brother Saul, Jesus himself who appeared to you has sent me so that you may regain your sight and be filled with the Holy Ghost."

All at once Saul could see again! He got up and was baptized. In this way Saul, the self-important man, became the Lord's most humble servant. Soon he was named Paul, which means "little".

Acts 9:1 - 20

Saul is blinded by a bright light from heaven.

Parents: *O taste and see that the Lord is good: blessed is the man that trusteth in him.* (Psalm 34:8)

Children: 1. Why did Saul go to Damascus?
2. What happened to Saul before he got there?
3. Who called out to him saying, "Saul, Saul"?

PETER'S VISION
Salvation for Everyone

One day while Peter was staying at Joppa, he went up on the flat roof of a house to pray. While there he fell into a dream-like trance. He saw heaven opened and something like a great sheet being let down by its four corners. Inside were many four-footed animals, reptiles, and birds -- some were clean and others unclean. The Old Testament law said the unclean should not be eaten.

Then a voice said, "Rise, Peter, kill and eat."

Peter was very hungry. But he said, "No, Lord, for I have never eaten anything unclean." This happened three times. Then the sheet went back up and disappeared. While Peter puzzled over this strange vision, the Spirit told him that three men were looking for him. So he went downstairs and found them.

The men said, "A God-fearing Roman centurion named Cornelius sent us to find you." Peter invited them to stay for the night. He planned to go back with them the next day along with six more men.

When the group arrived at Cornelius' house, a crowd of people had already gathered. Then Peter said, "You know it is against the Jewish law for me to enter a Gentile home like this. But God has showed me in a vision that we should never think ourselves better than anyone else. Now may I ask why you sent for me?"

Cornelius explained, "Four days ago I was fasting and praying. All at once a man appeared in bright clothing. He told me to send for you, and also gave directions where to find you. Now we are eager to hear your message from God."

Peter replied, "Truly God shows no favoritism for any nation, and the Jews are not His only people! But any man who does what is right and walks humbly before God may receive His salvation."

Then Peter told them the wonderful story of Jesus. He said that Jesus wanted everyone, both Jew and Gentile, to believe in Him.

While Peter was speaking all his listeners were filled with the Holy Spirit. This proved beyond a doubt that the Gentiles could also be a part of the true Christian Church.

Acts 10:1 - 38

Peter sees a sheet full of animals in a vision.

Parents: *For there is no difference between the Jew and the Greek; for the same Lord over all is rich unto all that call upon him.* (Romans 10:12)

Children:
1. Where was Peter when he had a vision?
2. Where did the sheet with animals come from?
3. What were the people called who were not Jews?

PETER IN PRISON
Freed by an Angel

All over Palestine, more and more people were becoming believers. The persecution had stopped for awhile and the churches were enjoying peace.

Then King Herod found out that the Jewish leaders liked him better when he mistreated the believers. He was especially popular for killing the apostle James with the sword. So the king singled out Peter as his next victim. On the first day of the Passover feast, Peter was arrested and put into prison. The king planned to wait until after the seven-day festival for his public trial.

During this whole week the desciples prayed day and night for Peter. Finally it was the last night, just before he was to die. Would God deliver him?

Inside the prison, four soldiers were guarding Peter around the clock. He was double-chained between two soldiers while the other two guarded the gates. There Peter slept as peacefully as a child.

Suddenly an angel stood beside him in a beam of glorious light. He tapped Peter's side and said, "Get up quickly!" The heavy chains dropped away. "Now put on your clothes and shoes, then follow me," said the angel.

Peter obeyed, thinking he was dreaming. They walked past the first guard, then the second one. Finally they reached the heavy iron gate which led to the city. It mysteriously opened by itself! The angel walked the length of one street with Peter, then he disappeared.

At last Peter realized what had happened. "It's really true!" he thought. "The angel of the Lord has rescued me from my enemies!"

Then Peter went straight to the prayer meeting. A girl named Rhoda answered his knock and immediately recognized his voice. Instead of opening the door, she ran to tell the good news to the others.

"You must be mad," the people said flatly. "No, I'm not," Rhoda declared. "It really is Peter!" "It is his angel," they insisted. But Peter kept knocking until they opened the door. How amazed they were to see him! They rejoiced to know that God truly does hear the prayers of His people.

Acts 12:1 - 19

An angel frees Peter from prison.

Parents: *Therefore I say unto you, what things soever ye desire, when ye pray, believe that ye receive them, and ye shall have them.* (Mark 11:24)

Children:
1. What did the disciples do while Peter was in prison?
2. Who rescued Peter from prison?
3. Who recognized Peter's voice?

PAUL AND SILAS IN PRISON

Singing in the Night

As the churches grew, the believers spread out farther from Jerusalem. Diligent missionaries were fulfilling Jesus' "great commission" to take the gospel to the whole world.

Paul and Silas traveled far away to Philippi in northern Greece. There they taught some people who often gathered beside a river to pray.

One day Paul and Silas met a slave girl who brought her masters much money by fortune-telling. It grieved Paul's heart to know that an evil spirit was working through her. So he told the evil spirit, "I command thee in the name of Jesus to come out of her." At once the spirit left her.

Now the girl's owners were angry because their source of easy money was gone. They seized Paul and Silas and dragged them to the judge. "These men are Jews," they cried. "They're stirring up trouble by teaching customs contrary to Roman laws."

Soon a mob joined the attack. Paul and Silas were whipped publicly and thrown into the innermost dungeon of the prison.

Paul and Silas were peaceful and happy in spite of their painful bruises and bleeding backs. At midnight they prayed and sang praises to the Lord. Never before had the other prisoners heard anything like this. It was the first "sacred concert" ever held in Europe! How Jesus' heart must have been touched.

Suddenly a violent earthquake shook the prison to its very foundations. Doors flew open and the chains of every prisoner fell off! Truly God was answering prayer. The jailor woke up and saw the open doors. He was terrified, thinking that the prisoners had escaped. Surely he would be blamed for carelessness. In despair he drew his sword to kill himself.

Then Paul called out, "Don't harm yourself for we are all here!" The jailor called for a light. He fell down before Paul and Silas, trembling. "What must I do to be saved?" he asked. "Believe on the Lord Jesus Christ, then you and your household will be saved," they replied.

What a night it was for the jailor and his family! After tending to the wounds of Paul and Silas, the whole family was baptized. Then a delicious meal was served with everyone rejoicing in their new faith in the Lord Jesus.

Acts 16:16 - 40

The jailor and his family rejoice in their new faith with Paul and Silas.

Parents: *That if thou shalt confess with thy mouth the Lord
Jesus, and shalt believe in thine heart that God hath
raised him from the dead, thou shalt be saved.*
(Romans 10:9)

Children: 1. When did Paul and Silas start singing?
2. Why was the jailor so scared?
3. What did Paul and Silas tell the jailor to do?

NEW JERUSALEM -- HEAVEN AND EARTH

Behold, I Make All Things New

John, called the disciple whom Jesus loved, lived to be an old man. Because he kept speaking about Jesus and preaching God's Word, the cruel emperor of Rome sent him away from Israel. He was banished to a barren, rocky island called Patmos.

One morning, on the Lord's day, John saw Jesus in a vision. Jesus told him, "Write in a book everything that you see." Then John saw the door of heaven itself opening. Inside someone was sitting on a throne encircled by a glowing rainbow. In His hand He held a book about the future. It was tightly sealed so that no man could open it.

Then Jesus took the book. He was the only person both able and worthy to open the seals. Immediately thousands upon thousands of angels and elders burst out singing, "Worthy is the Lamb that was slain to receive power and glory and blessing!"

Jesus opened the seals one by one. Each time John saw new things happening, but God was always in control of the whole world. Satan, the enemy of God, had plunged the world into sin and suffering. But Jesus defeated him for good when He died and rose again.

God put an end to every old thing that was ugly or spoiled. John heard Jesus say, "Behold, I make all things new." Then a new heaven and a new earth appeared, all perfect, lovely and good. Immediately the holy city, the new Jerusalem, came out of heaven as beautiful as a bride at her wedding.

After this John heard a voice saying, "God's home is with mankind, and He Himself will be with them. God will wipe away all tears. He will make an end of the sea and of the night. There will be no sorrow, crying, pain, or death anymore."

No more sea means no more separation, restlessness, or turmoil like the ocean waves.

No more night means no blindness, darkness, shadows, or nightmares.

No more sorrow means no troubles, disasters, sadness, threats, or trials.

No more crying means no anguish, distress, heartaches, or grief.

No more pain means no aches, misery, suffering, exhaustion, or torture.

No more death means no disease, decay, accidents, or loneliness.

John wrote, "Blessed are those who obey God's commandments, that they may enter in through the gates into the city."

"I am coming soon," said Jesus.

John answered for all believers the world over. "Amen. Come, Lord Jesus!"

Revelation 1:9 - 11, 4:1 - 3, 5:11 - 12, 21:1 - 27, 22:14

John sees the New Jerusalem coming down out of heaven.

Parents: *Wherefore we receiving a kingdom which cannot be moved, let us have grace, whereby we may serve God acceptably with reverence and godly fear.* (Hebrew 12:28)

Children: 1. Why was John put on an island alone?
2. Who sang in heaven as Jesus opened the book of the future?
3. Who will wipe away all tears?

213

Index of Scripture References

Dear Reader,

We hope you have enjoyed your copy of <u>101 Favorite Stories from the Bible</u>! This book was published by **Christian Aid Ministries**, which is headquartered in Berlin, Ohio, and was established in 1981 as a non-profit, tax-exempt 501(c)(3) organization to bring spiritual and material aid to the suffering church in communist Romania. **CAM** has since enlarged its work to include the former Soviet Union, Nicaragua and Haiti.

CAM is supported entirely by contributions from concerned individuals and church groups throughout the USA, Canada and a number of other countries. A large percentage of the support comes from Amish and conservative Mennonite donors; there is also substantial help from a wide range of other churches and non-denominational groups.

CAM's original purpose in publishing <u>101 Favorite Stories from the Bible</u> was to develop a children's Bible story book which was consistent with what we believe the Bible teaches. This book was to be printed in the Romanian, Russian, Spanish, and Haitian Creole languages, then distributed throughout various countries across the world. Much care was taken to make all the stories and illustrations as Biblically accurate as possible. In the process of writing this book, we became aware that there might be a market for these books in English and German. Thus, these books are now available for sale in all six languages from **TGS**, a wholly-owned subsidiary of Christian Aid Ministries. **Every retail copy of <u>101 Favorite Stories from the Bible</u> sold helps us distribute foreign language copies free-of-charge to the poor in other countries.**

If you are interested in buying another copy of <u>101 Favorite Stories from the Bible</u> in any language, fill out the form below. You are also welcome to subscribe to **CAM's** monthly newsletter. The newsletter is completely free and no obligations follow.

[] Yes, I would like to receive my free monthly copy of CAM's newsletter.

[] Yes, I would like to order _____ (qty) copies of **101 Favorite Stories from the Bible** - ___(qty) English, ___ German, ___ Spanish, ___ Romanian, ___ Russian and ___ Haitian Creole. Enclosed is my payment of $_____ ($12.99 per copy, plus $2.50 shipping and handling.) If buying more than one copy, please add an additional $.50 per copy for shipping and handling.

**Each retail copy purchased helps CAM
to distribute one foreign language copy to those in need.**

* All foreign orders: please write for your postage costs.
Bookstores and dealers, ask about our discount schedule.
Ohio residents, please add 6.25% tax to book total (no tax on shipping and handling).

Name_____

Address_____

City_____

State_____ Zip_____

Make checks payable to:

> **TGS International***
> **PO Box 355**
> **Berlin, OH 44610**
> **Telephone (330) 893-2428**

*TGS is a wholly-owned subsidiary of Christian Aid Ministries.